x507 M78y
Moore, W
Your science fair project

FE

YOUR SCIENCE FAIR PROJECT

Devoted to science fair projects for the third through the eighth grades, the book gives a detailed description of the materials and tools necessary and the actual steps for building a science project. Many of the materials are household items—cardboard boxes, toys, wire hangers—items within the reach of all readers. As the author suggests, curiosity about the "why" of things is the first step, and with the photographs and instructions given, you are on your way to a first-rate science fair project.

YOUR

SCIENCE FAIR

PROJECT

By WILLIAM MOORE

G. P. PUTNAM'S SONS NEW YORK

CONTENTS

ACKNOWLEDGMENTS

The author is indebted to several people for their help with this book. Mrs. Esther Marcus, who is an Elementary School Science Coordinator in New York City, made a number of important suggestions. Mr. Arthur Sheran, a teacher of science, was also very helpful, not only with advice but with materials necessary for the photographs. Another science teacher, Mr. Eli Slotkin, contributed a number of useful research materials, and Mr. Fred Erdin, an Industrial Arts teacher at the same school, Walt Whitman Junior High, supplied information and materials for photographs. Much of the typing and correspondence involved was done, as usual, by my wife Winifred.

Thanks are also due to the following young people who spent many hours helping with projects and posing for the photographs.

Gerald Altman	Jimmy Hubbert	Jo Ann Russello
Harvey Brandwein	Jimmy Maude	Arthur Semetis
Jo Chavis	Jonathan Moore	Espy Semetis
Craig Fuller	Kathleen Moore	Peter Semetis
George Hubbert	Diane Russello	Joseph Vitolo

YOUR
SCIENCE FAIR
PROJECT

"FINDING" YOUR PROJECT

Have you ever wondered why the leaves fall from trees, why the wind blows, and sometimes only candy seems sweet? What do you think causes airplanes to fly and spaceships to spin about the earth? Being curious about such things, or a thousand others, will help you to get started on a science project. Being willing to try out your ideas is important too.

In this book you will find many questions and many suggestions for finding the answers. When you have found an answer you will have a science project which you may want to enter in a science fair. The many instructions and photographs in this book will help you to get started and to complete your project. Of course, you may need some help, but try to find as many of the answers as you can yourself. It's more fun that way.

One other suggestion. Look through the entire book first. You may select a question from any part of this book. Investigate the question and work on the project which interests you most.

Finally, you may want to team up with a friend or classmate to find the answers to a question. If so, let him help you select the question as well as do the work.

9

WHERE TO FIND MATERIALS FOR PROJECTS

Don't overlook your own home as a place to find many of the materials and supplies you'll need. Cardboard boxes, for example, have many uses. A shallow one, particularly the bottom part, may be a good thing in which to display your entire project. With a pair of scissors you may also be able to cut out a large panel on which you can mount parts of your project. Corrugated boxes may also be used in the same way. Many of these can be painted with water colors or colored with crayons. You can paste or cement things to them. Tape and metal staples will also hold things to cardboard.

Wire clothes hangers, very light ones, are another item which have many uses. They can be cut with small nippers or common pliers. They can be easily bent into many shapes and colored with enamel or lacquer. Avoid the heavier, thicker ones however as they are more difficult to cut or bend.

You will find glass jars useful in two main ways. You may need a few in which to mix things, and occasionally they may be just what you need as a container in which to display your work. Tin cans, of course, are valuable in the same ways. Be sure they are clean and have no sharp edges.

A number of projects in this book require pieces of cloth. Here old and discarded clothing may solve your problem. When asking for pieces of discarded clothing you may want to ask for something of cotton, wool, silk, or rayon. If you are not sure about the kind of cloth you have, check with two or three people who know about such things.

A knowledge of toys and where to find them will be helpful too. Toys can provide the materials for several projects in this book. If it is necessary to take them apart, particularly the metal ones, ask for some help. Ask about the tools you may need and the safest way to proceed.

Don't forget about the garden, if you have one, or any of the living things around your house. Some of the projects you may want to work on require vegetables and flowers. Ask for permission and help, if necessary, before digging and removing them. Planting may require some help too. The trees and shrubs around your house may provide a supply of leaves and seeds for some of the experiments with living things. If you live in an apartment house, and there are no trees and shrubs around it, you may have to visit a friend or neighbor's house where some are located. Of course, ask permission before cutting parts of plants anywhere.

Among the living things which can be found around most houses are ants and other interesting insects. Collect them in clean milk cartons, or some similar container. Strange insects should not be handled with your bare hands at any time. Use a pair of tweezers or leave them alone until someone has identified them as safe to handle.

For a certain project you may wish to buy a piece of wood at the lumber yard. If so, there are a few facts you should know. One of these is that every board has two surfaces, two edges and two ends. When ordering you will want to state three measurements: the thickness, the width, and the length. The thickness refers to the distance between the two surfaces, the width to the distance between the two edges, and the length to the distance between the two ends. An order might look like this: $\frac{3}{4}'' \times 8'' \times 20''$. Here the $\frac{3}{4}''$ is the thickness, the $8''$ is the width, and the $20''$ is the length. Soft woods, such as white pine, poplar, basswood, and spruce, are easily sawed, planed, and sanded. These are also the less expensive woods and the best ones for a beginner to use. If you do not want knots or knotholes in your finished project, ask for clear boards.

You may wish to buy a small piece of metal too. This can be bought at your local sheetmetal shop, hardware store, or craft supply house. Galvanized iron, black iron, tinplate, aluminum, and copper may be purchased in sheet form. They are made and sold according to their thickness or weight. Each thickness of sheet metal has a number which is called the gage number. The gage number is taken from a measuring tool called a sheetmetal gage. The important thing to remember is that the numbers and thicknesses run from 0 to 36. The higher the number, the thinner the metal. Metals which are thinner than 36 gage are usually called foils. These are generally available in craft and hobby stores.

Most of the electrical materials which you may need for a project can be secured from the local hardware store. Bell wire or annunciator wire and batteries can be purchased quite inexpensively. Avoid buying things you don't really need or unnecessary amounts by making a list before you go to the store and then having someone check the list with you.

In general, try to locate the materials you need in and around your own home before going to a store. Look in closets and other storage places, such as an attic, basement, or garage, first. Don't hesitate to ask for help in your search for supplies and, of course, try to collect all the materials you will need before going on with your experiment.

PROJECTS FOR THE THIRD, FOURTH AND FIFTH GRADES

What Do You Think?

How must you take care of a pet?
(Use your own dog, cat, bird, turtle, mice, or any
other pet you may have at home.)

Finding the Answer

1. Make a list of things that must be done for a pet.
2. Do some or all of these things for your pet.
3. Find pictures in magazines of the things on your list and cut them out.
4. Ask your parents and friends for suggestions about things to add to your list.
5. If possible, ask someone to show your list to a man in a pet store. Have them ask him if it is a good list.

Showing Your Answers at the Science Fair

1. Paste a photograph of your pet on a large piece of heavy cardboard or paper.

13

2. On the same cardboard or paper paste magazine pictures of some of the things your pet needs.
3. Number and name everything on your board or paper.

New Questions

Do all pets need the same things?
How might your list change from winter to summer?

What Do You Think?

What sounds are made by people at work?

Finding the Answer

1. Listen to the sounds made by men working in the street. Hear the sounds made by men building a house. Notice the sounds made by a shoemaker, a baker, and a tailor.
2. Make a list of the sounds and the kinds of people who make them.
3. Ask your parents and others about the words which describe the work of firemen, policemen, and others.

Showing Your Answers at the Science Fair

1. Title a notebook or a folder with the words: "The Sounds of People Working."
2. Find pictures, in newspapers and magazines, of people working.
3. Cut and paste the pictures you have found in your notebook or folder.
4. Number and name each picture. Write the word which describes the sounds in each picture.

New Questions

Does every kind of work make sounds?
What kind of work makes the least sound?
Note: Here are some other titles for similar projects:
        The Sounds of a Baseball Game;
        Sounds Heard on a Playground;
        Sounds Heard on the Way to School.

What Do You Think?

Can a musical instrument be made with rubber bands?

Finding the Answer

1. Locate two or three empty milk cartons.
2. Cut a different sized opening in each carton with a pair of household scissors.
3. Stretch two or three rubber bands around the cartons and over the openings. Also place a crayon or pencil under the rubber bands at one end of the carton. Which location produces the best tones?
4. Stretch rubber bands over a ruler lengthwise. Use a pencil as a bridge.
5. Locate a small box in which a hole may be cut. Stretch rubber bands around this and see what tones are produced.

Showing Your Answers at the Science Fair

1. Show several instruments you have made.
2. Explain in writing which arrangement of holes, rubber bands and bridges produced the most musical tones.

New Questions

How does the size of the opening and the location of the bridge affect the sounds?

How do the size and the tightness of the rubber bands affect the sounds?

What Do You Think?

Is a compass like a magnet?

Finding the Answer

1. Locate a small bar or pencil-shaped magnet. These can be purchased as a part of an inexpensive toy at most toy stores.
2. Float the small magnet on a sliver of light wood in an aluminum pan or a wooden bowl.
3. Place a compass near the bowl and look to see if the magnet floats in the same position as the needle of the compass.

Showing Your Answers at the Science Fair

1. Mark the words "north," "south," "east" and "west" in the right places on the edge of the pan or bowl.
2. Show your bowl with the floating magnet. Place a compass next to the bowl.
3. Explain in writing how the magnet acts like a compass.

New Questions

In what other ways can a magnet be used?
Why is a compass a useful thing?

What Do You Think?

In what directions does the street in front of your house run?

Finding the Answer

1. Locate a compass, a ruler, and a large sheet of paper.
2. Draw a circle slightly larger than your compass near the center of the paper. Draw a long line through the center of the circle and along the length of the paper.
3. Lay the paper on the sidewalk in front of your house so that the long line runs in the same direction as the sidewalk.
4. Place the compass in the circle on the paper and turn it until North is located at the point of the needle. Now the compass will tell you the directions of the long line on the paper. Mark these directions on the paper at the ends of the line.

Showing Your Answers at the Science Fair

1. Use the paper you have drawn the long line on and make a small map showing the nearby streets, your house, grocery store, school, etc. Mark the main compass points on the edge of the circle already drawn on the paper.
2. Show the map you have made and explain in writing how it was made.

New Questions

Why do some streets have the words "north," "south," "east" and "west" as
    part of their names?
Does the sun rise exactly in the east and set exactly in the west?

What Do You Think?

How much cooler is it in the shade than in the sun?

Finding the Answer

1. Ask your parents for an inexpensive thermometer.
2. Learn how to read a thermometer. Your teacher or any adult can help
    you learn.
3. Place the thermometer in the shade of a building for about ten minutes.
    Use a watch to time this and then mark the level of the liquid in the ther-
    mometer on the face of it with a pen, pencil or a scratched line. A rubber
    band stretched around the thermometer will also serve as a marker.
4. Next, place the thermometer in the sun for an equal amount of time and
    then mark the level of the liquid in the same way.

Showing Your Answers at the Science Fair

1. Tape your thermometer to a large sheet of cardboard or a piece of wood.
2. Use a pen or a dark pencil to show the different temperatures you re-
    corded.
3. Use pictures cut from magazines and papers to show the uses of shade.

New Questions

Are all shady spots the same temperature?
Are the differences greater on very hot days?

Finding the Answer

1. Make a rain catcher with a coffee can and a ruler. Wedge the ruler into the coffee can with a small stick.
2. Drive a stake into the ground in an open spot and tie the can to the stake. This will hold the can in place.
3. Keep a written record of the rainfall on several days. Mark the amounts on a calendar.

Showing Your Answers at the Science Fair

1. Show your rain catcher.
2. Paste your calendar page to a heavy piece of cardboard.
3. Add to the cardboard some newspaper accounts of the rainfalls which you measured.

New Questions

Why were the amounts you measured sometimes different from the amounts forecast in the newspapers?

In what kind of device does the weather bureau catch and measure the rainfall?

What Do You Think?

Of what is snow made?

Finding the Answer

1. Place an empty coffee can outdoors in an open spot. Do this just before a snowfall.
2. After the snowfall, measure the depth of the snow in the can with a ruler.
3. Take the can of snow indoors and allow the snow to melt. Measure the liquid content with a ruler.
4. Find out why there is less water than snow in the can. Try packing some

snow down tightly in the can to make it occupy less space. Why is this possible?

5. Strain the water from the melted snow through a cloth. What do you find accompanies the snow?

Showing Your Answers at the Science Fair

1. Show your snow collector and the ruler with which you measured the snow and water. Show the cloth you used to strain the water.
2. Explain in writing exactly what you did and what you discovered. Do this in step-by-step fashion and give the dates and times.

New Questions

Does the same amount of water always come from the same amount of snow? Does some dirt fall with a snow or only afterwards?

What Do You Think?

How does a wind vane tell us the direction of the wind?

Finding the Answer

1. Look at any wind vanes which may be on buildings in your neighborhood. Note in what direction they point.
2. Check your findings with an adult.
3. Make your own wind vane. This can be in the shape of an airplane, an arrow, a rocket, on a sheet of corrugated cardboard. Make sure that one end of it is much larger than the other.
4. After cutting out the rocket or arrow, thread a string through the middle of it and tie a knot or button underneath. The knot or button will prevent it from slipping down.
5. Hold this with your hands or tie it to something higher in the air.
6. Keep a written record of the wind direction on several days.

Showing Your Answers at the Science Fair

1. Show your own wind vane and explain in writing how it was made and used.

19

2. Draw some squares on a sheet of paper. Indicate that each square stands for one day. Write inside each square the wind direction and time of day.

New Questions

Are the clouds high in the sky always moving in the same direction as the clouds closer to the ground?

From what direction do the strongest winds seem to come?

What Do You Think?

How can we show the speed of the wind?

Finding the Answer

1. Make a whirl-a-gig from heavy paper.
2. Nail or pin it on the end of a long stick.
3. Color one of the points of the whirl-a-gig so that the number of turns can be counted.
4. Count the number of turns in three seconds or five seconds. Do this at different times on more than one day. Have a friend with a clock or watch tell you when to start and stop counting.

Showing Your Answers at the Science Fair

1. Show your whirl-a-gig and explain how it was used.
2. Display a record you have kept of the wind speed on several occasions.
3. Mount some newspaper accounts of the wind speed on a piece of cardboard.

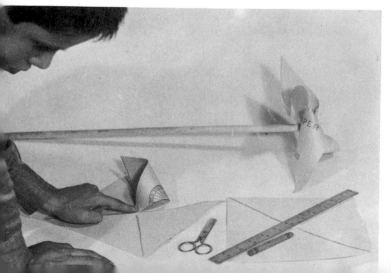

Attach your whirl-a-gig loosely to the top of a stick as shown here. Try to count the number of revolutions in two or three seconds. You may need a friend to watch the clock and tell you when to count.

New Questions

Was the wind strongest on sunny or on cloudy days?
Was it usually windy before a rain?

What Do You Think?

What is wind?

Finding the Answer

1. Blow up a balloon and then let out the air. Feel the air moving over your hands and face.
2. Fan yourself with a piece of paper. What do you feel?
3. Notice what the wind does to trees and how it feels on your face.
4. Have someone help you fly a kite. Why is it sometimes hard to hold the kite string in your hands?

Showing Your Answers at the Science Fair

1. Cut pictures from papers and magazines which show how the air moves.
2. Make crayon drawings of things moved by the air.
3. Cut out pictures of things which cause the air to move, such as balloons and fans.
4. Paste your pictures and drawings in a special booklet or on a large sheet of cardboard. Number and name each picture.

New Questions

How can you tell when the air is moving fast?
Does the air ever move too fast?

What Do You Think?

What things will the wind carry farthest?

Finding the Answer

1. Take two sheets of paper, of equal size. Crumple one piece of paper into a tight ball. Drop both pieces from a porch or a low window on a windy day. Note which travels farther.

2. Fold some notebook paper into gliders. Shape each one differently. Discover which of them will travel farthest in a wind.
3. Find some seeds from a maple or a catalpa tree (or any other plant) and drop them on a windy day. Notice which travels farthest.

Showing Your Answers at the Science Fair

1. Tape the leaves, seeds, and gliders you dropped in the wind to a sheet of cardboard. Arrange and number them so that people can see which ones traveled farthest.
2. List all the seeds, leaves, and gliders you have tested and indicated the exact distance each traveled when dropped.
3. Explain in writing what you have done and what you have discovered.

New Questions

Does the shape of an object help it to travel farther in the wind?
Does the weight of an object have much to do with the distance it will travel?

Why will some leaves fly farther in the wind than others? Crumple one sheet of paper into a ball and make another into an airplane. See which one will be carried farthest by the wind. Keep a record of the distances.

What things are shaped best for rolling? Test your guesses by actually rolling things down the same slope and then measuring the distance they roll. Mark a number on each round object and then record the distance it rolls.

What Do You Think?

What shapes roll best?

Finding the Answer

1. Collect a number of small objects which might roll, such as a ball, a marble, a top, a pencil, a spool, a button, etc.
2. Raise one end of a sheet of corrugated cardboard or piece of wood and allow it to rest on some books or another board.
3. Roll each object down this cardboard or wooden ramp and mark where it stops rolling. Measure and record the distances.

Showing Your Answers at the Science Fair

1. Show your ramp and the objects you tested.
2. Number and name each of the rolled objects on a sheet of paper. Indicate the distance each rolled.
3. Explain in writing why you think certain objects rolled farther than others.

New Questions

Do big things roll better than small things?
Do heavier things roll better than light things?

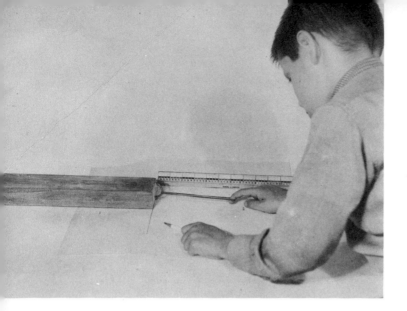

Over what surfaces will this block of wood slide easiest? Avoid guessing by using a ruler and a rubber band such as those shown here. Place the block on several surfaces and measure the stretch before the block moves.

What Do You Think?

Over what surfaces will things slide easiest?

Finding the Answer

1. Drive a nail into a small block of wood and attach a rubber band to the nail. This may also be done by slipping a string through a rubber band and then tying the string around a book.
2. Use a ruler or a tape measure to measure the distances the rubber band stretches as it begins to pull ·or move the block over different surfaces.
3. Pull the block or book over a wooden floor, a tile floor, a rug, sandpaper, cloth, a sidewalk, etc.

Showing Your Answers at the Science Fair

1. Show your test block or book with the attached rubber band. Explain in writing how the block or book was used and how the measurement was made.
2. Make a chart which shows the kinds of surfaces tested and how far the rubber band stretched on each test.

New Questions

Would the results be the same if a heavier block or book were used?
How could some surfaces be made smoother?

What Do You Think?

How can things be made to slide more easily?

Finding the Answer

1. Make a testing device with a clean board which is more than a foot long. Rest one end of the board on something at least eight or ten inches high.
2. Locate some wooden play blocks which are the same in size and shape.
3. See how far down the board one of the blocks will slide and mark the distance with a pencil.
4. Apply some soap and water to the bottom side of a block and mark the distance it will slide. Remove the soap with steel wool and a rag. Then repeat the test using, in turn, wax, oil, Vaseline, and other lubricants. Mark and record the distance reached with each lubricant.

How can we make things slide more easily? Create a sharp incline as shown here and measure the distance the blocks will slide. Try several lubricants, such as soap, wax and oil, to see which will make it slide farthest.

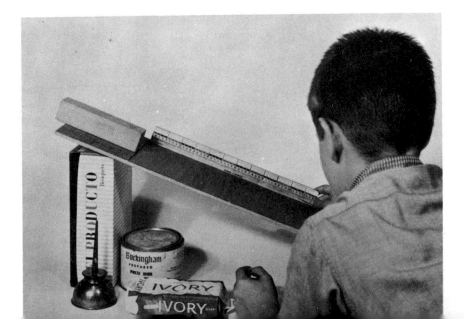

Showing Your Answers at the Science Fair

1. Show your testing device and all of the lubricants you have tested.
2. Make a chart showing how far the blocks slide on each trial.
3. Explain how friction holds things back and how lubricants help to keep them moving.

New Questions

When is friction helpful?
When is friction not useful?
Where are lubricants applied to bicycles, roller skates, wagons, and carriages?

What Do You Think?

In how many ways can we make things go upward?

Finding the Answer

1. Build a catapult using a stick, two blocks of wood, and nails.
2. Make a rubber band slingshot.
3. Make a rubber band powered airplane.
4. Use a spring to propel things upward.
5. Discover other ways to make things go upward.

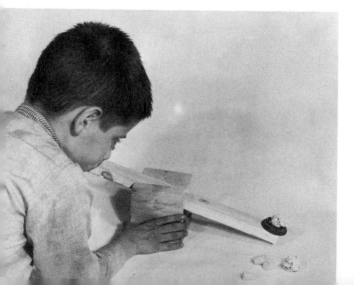

You'll need three pieces of wood to make this catapult. It is only one device which will make things go upward. How many other devices can you think of which will help to make things go up? Can you build them?

Showing Your Answers at the Science Fair

1. Name and number each of the devices you have built.
2. Explain in writing which devices worked best.
3. Show some magazine and newspaper pictures of rockets and missiles which are being used to propel men and to carry explosives.
4. Show some toys or pictures of toys which make things go upward. These could include a jack-in-the-box, model cannon, airplanes, etc.
5. Explain, if you can, why most things fall back to the earth.

New Questions

Since our earth is like a ball in shape, and people live all over its surface, what do the words UP and DOWN really mean?

Is the old saying, "What goes up must come down," true?

What Do You Think?

Does the sun seem to follow a similar path each day?

Finding the Answer

1. Locate the sun in the sky at 9, 12, and 3 o'clock on several days. Be sure

Does the sun follow nearly the same path each day? Exactly where is the sun each day at twelve o'clock? Use a crayon and a large sheet of paper to make a picture which shows where the sun is located each hour of the day.

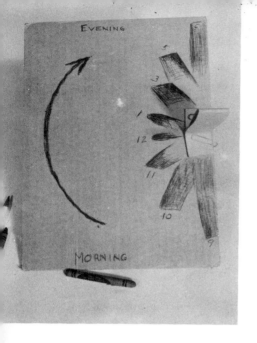

Here is a cardboard sun clock. Why can't this clock be used every day? Why would a new one have to be made every few weeks? A long pencil could also be substituted for the vertical piece of cardboard on the right edge.

to stand in the same spot each day and note a building or tree directly under the sun.

2. Place a stick in the ground and mark the tip of the shadows with stones on several days.

3. Draw a house to represent your home on the bottom edge of a piece of cardboard. Then draw circles to represent the sun at various hours of the day. Use crayons if you wish and mark the times of the day you saw the sun in those places.

Showing Your Answers at the Science Fair

1. Display your cardboard picture. Tape or paste another piece of cardboard to the back so that the picture will stand on edge.

2. Explain in writing exactly what you have done and what you have learned.

New Questions

Where is the sun during our night time?

Why doesn't the moon give as much light as the sun?

What Do You Think?

Can the sun's shadow help us to tell time?

Finding the Answer

1. Fasten a pencil or a piece of cardboard upright on a sheet of corrugated board.
2. Place this on a windowsill or wherever the sun is shining.
3. Mark the location of the shadow of the upright piece each hour. Indicate the time at the tip of each shadow.
4. Return this clock to the same spot and place it in the same position on another day. Is the sun clock accurate?

Showing Your Answers at the Science Fair

1. Show your sun clock.
2. Explain in writing how the clock was made and what you think are its weaknesses.

New Questions

Why were the shadows shorter around noontime than during the morning and afternoon hours?

Why won't this clock work every day?

What Do You Think?

How much of the earth is in sunlight and how much in darkness?

Finding the Answer

1. Since the earth is shaped somewhat like a ball you can place a large ball in the bright sunlight to see how much of it is covered with sunlight.
2. Shine a flashlight on a ball in a darkened room. Try this with a candle, too, instead of a flashlight.
3. If one is available, use a geographic globe in the same way.
4. Compare your results with the pictures found in a geography book or encyclopedia.

Showing Your Answers at the Science Fair

1. Cut a hole in the lid of a cigar box or a similar sized container. Mount a small globe in the middle of a wire and opposite the hole in the box. The small globes can be purchased in a toy or ten-cent store. Use a pen or pocket flashlight to throw a light beam on the globe. The inside of the box should be painted black.
2. Explain in writing how the sun creates daylight. Explain what is happening in those areas of the globe which are neither completely light or completely dark. Explain why each day lasts twenty-four hours.

New Questions

Why is it generally hotter near the equator than at the poles?
How does sunlight cause changes in our weather?

What Do You Think?

How is concrete made and used?
(This can also be done with plaster and sandpaper, for example.)

Finding the Answer

1. If possible, watch men at work who are building a concrete wall, walk, or driveway. Ask what they are mixing.
2. Ask parents or relatives who do such work for information.

This small metal globe and a pocket flashlight can be used to show exactly how much of the earth is in sunlight and how much in darkness. Run a small wire through the globe and also through both sides of the box to hold it in place.

2 25¢ **EL PRODUCTO**
Bouquets

You can make some things of concrete quite easily. Try mixing one spoonful of cement with two of sand and then three of gravel. Add enough water and mix until the batch is thick, like mashed potatoes.

3. Ask your parents to help you get a small amount of cement. A cigarboxful will do. Also locate a small amount each of sand and gravel.
4. Mix some cement, sand, and water in different proportions to see what happens. Add some gravel to a few batches.

Showing Your Answers at the Science Fair

1. Make two or three small objects of concrete, such as paperweights, statues, and book ends. Use cardboard boxes or holes in the ground as molds.
2. Paint these objects different colors when they are dry.
3. Explain in writing how concrete is mixed.
4. Cut from magazines and papers pictures of things made of concrete. Paste these pictures in a booklet or notebook to display them.

New Questions

How is mortar different from concrete?
What is "ready-mix"?

Finding the Answer

1. If possible, watch some men making a sidewalk. Note the order in which certain things are done.
2. Ask any adult who might know about such things.
3. Locate someone who has a bag of cement and ask him for a cup or two of it.
4. Measure out three tablespoons of cement and six tablespoons of sand. Mix these thoroughly and then add a tablespoon of water at a time until the batch becomes wetly thick, like mashed potatoes.
5. Place this batch of concrete into an empty milk carton and allow it to harden.
6. Mix another batch in the same manner but add some gravel. Spoon this into an open container too and allow it to harden.
7. When both batches are dry remove them from the boxes and examine

Plaster, the same kind that is used to make the smooth walls of houses, can be used to make many other things. You need only mix it with water until it is thick. Then just pour or spoon it into a mold.

them with a magnifying glass. Also, hit them with a hammer and let them soak in water overnight.

8. Compare both batches with a real sidewalk. Are they similar in appearance and hardness?

Showing Your Answers at the Science Fair

1. Show several pieces of the concrete you have made using different mixtures of cement, sand, gravel and water.
2. Explain in writing how each was made and which you think would make the best sidewalk.
3. Collect some interesting pictures of things made with concrete or of the tools, machinery, and equipment used in making a sidewalk.
4. List the steps followed by men in making a real sidewalk.

New Questions

When was concrete first used?
How long will concrete last?

Mount the labels from food packages on a large sheet of cardboard such as this one. Use rubber cement to attach them and crayons to print the additional information. A dark border can be added to the cardboard later.

What Do You Think?

Where do our breakfast foods come from?

Finding the Answer

1. List the foods you often eat for breakfast.
2. Find out which of the foods come from plants and which from animals. Ask adults and look in reference books for this information.
3. Discover what you can about the changes made in foods before we eat them. Consult some cookbooks and an encyclopedia.

Showing Your Answers at the Science Fair

1. On a large piece of cardboard mount pictures, photos, or names of foods cut from food wrappers or containers.
2. Under each picture or name tell if it came from a plant or an animal. Tell what changes were made in it so that it could be eaten.
3. Explain why you think each one is a good food.

New Questions

Do all foods come from either plants or animals?
Why are so many foods cooked?

What Do You Think?

Why are rocks sometimes used in building a house?

Finding the Answer

1. Collect several kinds of rocks. Find out what happens to them when they are left in water overnight, hit with a hammer or placed under a heavy object. Number each rock and record what happens to it during each test.
2. Look at several houses which have rock foundations, porches, fireplaces, or patios. Note and record the size and shape of the rocks used in each place.
3. If possible, ask a stone or brick mason why stones are used.
4. Look in reference books for information about the kinds of rocks used in buildings and statues.

Showing Your Answers at the Science Fair

1. Show your collection of rocks and explain in writing exactly what you did and what you discovered.
2. Use pictures and drawings cut from magazines to show the many uses of rocks.
3. Explain how rocks are often held together with mortar and how this is mixed.

New Questions

Why aren't rocks used in all buildings?
Where do rocks come from?

What Do You Think?

Where do buttons come from?

Finding the Answer

1. Collect some interesting buttons. Collect some buttons of different materials and design.
2. Ask a number of adults to tell you of what the buttons are made.
3. Find out more about these materials by looking in reference books at the library.

Showing Your Answers at the Science Fair

1. Sew or paste your buttons to a sheet of light cardboard.
2. Number and name each button. Explain the material from which it is made.
3. Show, on a piece of cloth attached to a cardboard, how buttons are sewed to fabric.

New Questions

Are other fasteners taking the place of buttons?
Where were buttons first used and what were they like?
Why do some buttons dissolve in a dry-cleaning machine?

Finding the Answer

1. Notice what happens to a particular puddle of water on the sidewalk over a period of one day. If necessary, pour a bit of water on a sunlit portion of sidewalk.
2. Pour some water in a can. Measure it carefully each day until it has disappeared.
3. Pour some water into a large jar. Do not fill the jar. Cover it with a saucer and place it in the sunlight. After a while see if you can find water drops collecting on the saucer. How do you think the water drops get to the saucer?
4. Ask some adults the name of the process by which water gets into the air. Look in reference books for more information about this process.

Showing Your Answers at the Science Fair

1. Exhibit your jar and saucer with each day's water level marked on the jar.
2. Show a calendar on which you have marked the amounts of water which went into the air each day.
3. Explain in writing how the water gets into the air and then into the saucer.

New Questions

On what kinds of days did the water seem to disappear faster?
Can we ever see water in the air?

PROJECTS FOR THE FOURTH, FIFTH AND SIXTH GRADES

What Do You Think?

What changes occur in a young pet during a one-month (or two-week) period?

Finding the Answer

1. If possible, study a newly acquired pet of your own, or one belonging to a friend.
2. Weigh your pet every day during this period. If your pet is very small use a postal scale. Also weigh the food given to the pet daily. If possible, even weigh and record what the pet has not eaten. Also, measure the water consumed.
3. Record in a notebook the date, time, and place of each feeding. Record the exact amounts of food and water consumed. Record the general appearance of the pet, his alertness and activity.

Showing Your Answers at the Science Fair

1. Mount a photograph of your pet on a large sheet of cardboard.

2. Make a chart which shows the date, time and amount of food consumed. Indicate weight and size changes too.
3. Explain in writing exactly what you have done and what you have discovered.

New Questions

Would a longer period of observation produce more interesting results?
What would an observed winter period as contrasted to a summer period show?

What Do You Think?

Should wild animals be protected?

Finding the Answer

1. Make a list of the wild animals you have seen in your neighborhood or in the nearby countryside. Your list may be easier to make if you will first find the meanings of the words "wild" and "animal" in your dictionary.

In how many ways is your pet growing and changing? This is Brownie, who grew to be twenty inches high (at the shoulder), and to weigh 60 pounds in one year. His ears did not stand until he was nine months old.

PROJECTS FOR THE FIFTH, SIXTH AND SEVENTH GRADES

What Do You Think?

Are many things still moved by human muscle?

Finding the Answer

1. Make a list of the things you know are moved by human muscle. Include such things as bicycles, wagons, pencil sharpeners, hammers, wrenches, etc.
2. Examine each thing on the list to see if it also has a belt, pulley, wheel, lever, screw, or some other device for helping human muscle. Remove those that do not.
3. Make a separate list of things that are moved by human muscle alone. Include such things as books being carried home from school, berries being picked, fruit from trees, groceries, a baby being carried, and dishes being set on the table.
4. Discover in reference books the names of some of the bigger muscles of the body. Find out how they are attached to the bone and how movement takes place.

Showing Your Answers at the Science Fair

1. Exhibit both lists and use pictures cut from magazines to show the kinds of work being done by human muscle.
2. If possible, show a drawing of the human body which presents some of the muscles used in work. If possible, also show how muscles are connected to the bones of the body.
3. Explain in writing exactly what you have done on this project and what you have learned.

New Questions

How much of the world's work is still done by human muscle?
What does the word "automation" mean?

Do lightness or darkness, dryness or wetness, dust and air have anything to do with creating bread mold? You can check for the presence of mold with a magnifying glass and then watch it grow.

What Do You Think?

Why does bread get moldy?

Finding the Answer

1. Cut several small cubes of bread and place them in separate saucers.
2. Cover one cube with a glass and add a few drops of water under the edge of the glass. Place this one in a dark closet. Examine the bread with a magnifying glass at least once a day for a week.
3. Rub one of the cubes of bread in dust before covering with glass and adding water. Observe daily.
4. Place one clean piece of bread under glass but add no water. Place this one also in a closet and observe daily.
5. Add water to another cube of bread, cover with a glass and allow it to stand in the sunlight for several days. Observe daily.
6. Place one cube of bread under a glass and inside a refrigerator. Observe daily.
7. Record daily in writing what has happened to each cube of bread. From your record see if you have evidence to indicate why bread gets moldy. Check your findings with your teacher.

Showing Your Answers at the Science Fair

1. Exhibit one of your saucers, a glass, bread cube, and a magnifying glass.
2. Show your written record of what happened daily to each piece of bread. Include the date, time and location of each piece.

New Questions

Are all molds undesirable?
Will molds grow on all foods?

83

What Do You Think?

Why are foods packaged in different kinds of containers?

Finding the Answer

1. Collect samples of several kinds of containers. Find boxes, cloth and paper bags, waxed cartons, pails, aluminum foil and plastic containers.
2. Test each container to find if it will:

   a. hold water,
   b. keep water out,
   c. hold heavy contents,
   d. keep out germs,

   e. break easily,
   f. tear easily,
   g. make contents visible,
   h. be disposable.

Showing Your Answers at the Science Fair

1. Exhibit samples of the containers. This can also be parts of containers and even labels from them.
2. Number each container and list its qualities. Show why it is a good container.
3. Explain in writing exactly what you did and what you discovered.

New Questions

Why must moisture and air be kept out of certain containers?
What suggestions do you have for improving certain containers?

What Do You Think?

Where can we find molds?

Finding the Answer

1. Rub some cut pieces of potato, orange, cheese, bread, and apple in dust and examine them once or twice a day with a magnifying glass. A small section may also be placed under a microscope and studied. Look for changes in the dust particles and the appearance of new materials.
2. Examine each piece until some mold has appeared. Record the date and time of appearance of each mold.

3. Place some of the mold from each piece of food on a separate sheet of white paper and examine it with a magnifying glass. Note the color, size, texture and design of each kind of mold. This may also be done under a microscope.

Showing Your Answers at the Science Fair

1. Exhibit samples of the food and the mold grown on each. These may be taped inside a box and labeled.
2. Show your magnifying glass and your record of observations.
3. Present in writing your description of each mold and how long each took to grow. Explain what you have done and what you have learned as a result of this experiment.

New Questions

Do all molds spoil food?
What conditions are required to produce mold?

What Do You Think?

Do many of our foods come from animals?

Finding the Answer

1. List all the things you can remember having eaten in one week's time.
2. Mark all of those which you know come from animals. Indicate which animal each comes from.
3. Now investigate the sources of all the other foods on your list. You may ask your parents, your school dietician, a nurse, a doctor and a grocer. Also consult reference books in your library.

Showing Your Answers at the Science Fair

1. On a large sheet of paper or in a special folder place pictures of the foods you have eaten in one week. Next to each picture write the name of the animal from which it comes. If the food comes from a plant, write the name of the plant.
2. Summarize in writing what you have done and what you have discovered.

New Questions

Could we live without food from animals?
Could we live without food from plants?

What Do You Think?

Of what are food containers made?

Finding the Answer

1. Use an old tin can to experiment. Scratch a can with a sharp tool or nail on both the inside and outside. Examine the scratched places with a magnifying glass. Allow the can to stay outdoors for a few days. Re-examine the can. If possible, inspect a can which has been in a bonfire and has had the coatings burned away. Investigate in reference books to discover the nature of the coatings on tin cans.
2. Scratch a milk container to discover its composition. Tear one apart and examine its edges. If possible, and you have permission, take one outdoors and burn it. Notice how it burns and what odors it gives off. Find in reference books the composition of milk containers.
3. Examine a glass bottle. Compare it with window glass and plate glass. Find the formulas used in making glass.
4. Collect some of the metals which are used to wrap candy, and some foods. Are these all aluminum, or are some tin foil?

Showing Your Answers at the Science Fair

1. Exhibit samples of various containers and explain how you tested them and what you discovered.
2. Make a large chart which shows all the materials you know are used in containers. Explain why you think each is used.
3. Explain in writing everything you have done and what you have discovered.

New Questions

What problems make food packaging difficult?
What would life be like without packaged foods?

What Do You Think?

Where do the foods from which we get energy to work and play come from?

Finding the Answer

1. Select a number of common foods, such as milk, eggs, bread, beef, cheese, and fish, and find out where each of these comes from. Trace each food to its origin.
2. Make a chart showing, for example, that milk comes from cows, and that cows must eat green plants. Name the plants. Do this with each food.

Showing Your Answers at the Science Fair

1. Make a picture chart which shows the picture of each food, its name, origin and composition.
2. Make a display card showing the name of each food and presenting its composition and origin.
3. Display a map which you have marked to show the origin of many foods geographically.

New Questions

Do all animals get energy from green plants?
What foods give us the most energy?

What Do You Think?

How is sound obtained from a phonograph record?

Finding the Answer

1. Hold a straight pin lightly on a turning 78-rpm record. What kind of sounds can be heard? Why are they not very clear?
2. Stick a straight pin through the corner of a postcard or index card and hold the card so that the pinpoint rides in the grooves of the turning record. Is this a better method of producing sound than the above method? If so, why?
3. Make a paper horn and stick the pin through the small or pinpointed end of the horn. Now hold the horn so that the point of the pin rides in

the grooves of the record. Use a magnifying glass to observe the vibrations. Why does the horn seem to help in producing more understandable sounds.

Showing Your Answers at the Science Fair

1. Attach your pins, card, and horn, along with an old phonograph record and the magnifying glass, to a large sheet of heavy cardboard. Number and name each item.
2. Explain in writing exactly what you did and what you discovered. Tell what the paper horn did and what the speaker does in a phonograph or radio.

New Questions

How does electricity help a phonograph?
Why are more than one speaker used in some phonographs and radios?

What Do You Think?

How do we hear things?

Finding the Answer

1. Hold one hand over one ear first; then hold both hands over both ears.
2. Next have someone hold his hands over both of your ears while you are touching a radio cabinet. Have another friend turn the radio on and off while your eyes are closed. What do you feel?
3. Place some salt or tiny pieces of paper on a drum and then turn on a nearby radio loudly. Notice what happens to the salt or bits of paper.
4. Locate a drawing in a reference book of the human ear. Notice how it is constructed and senses vibrations.
5. Identify several sounds with your eyes closed by remembering what made the sounds.

Showing Your Answers at the Science Fair

1. Trace or draw a picture of the human ear on a large piece of paper. Name each part and indicate its function. On the same paper draw the drum and the radio cabinet. Indicate how you used each of these.

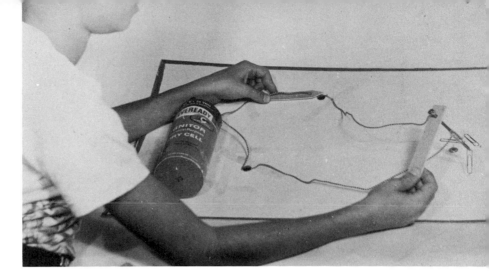

This electromagnet was made by wrapping some bell wire around a nail and connecting both ends to a battery. One wire was then cut and a piece of cardboard attached to make a switch. See what it will pick up.

2. Show a few devices for creating sounds, such as a xylophone, drum, whistle, etc. Explain how vibrations created by these devices is sensed by the human ear.

New Questions

Can some vibrations damage the human ear?
Can the human ear sense all vibrations?
Why can dogs hear sounds that humans cannot?

What Do You Think?

Can electricity create magnetism?

Finding the Answer

1. Assemble two #6 dry-cell batteries, one 2-inch nail, a switch, and three feet of annunciator wire.
2. Wrap one piece of wire around the nail about eight times. Connect one end of this wire to the switch and the other end to one battery. Use the other wire to connect the other pole of the switch to both batteries. In this way you'll have a complete circuit.

3. Experiment with the number of turns around the nail to find which number makes the strongest magnet. Try to pick up paper clips, tacks, nails, hairpins, etc.

Showing Your Answers at the Science Fair

1. Mount your electromagnet on a board with wire or tape so that people can use the nail to pick up objects.
2. Explain in writing how you think electricity creates magnetism.

New Questions

Will one battery work as well as two?
What will happen if you change the size of the nail?

What Do You Think?

How does electricity make a motor turn or spin?

Finding the Answer

1. Wrap a long piece of bell wire around a nail and connect one end of the wire to a #6 dry-cell battery.

You can use this device to show how a motor works. Of course, in a motor it is electricity that creates the magnetism and not a hand magnet which Joseph is holding here. What part of a motor acts the same as the paper clips?

2. Use a large lump of clay to hold a pencil upright. Rest the center point of a cardboard disc on the pencil point. On the edge of the disc slip four paper clips, each a quarter of a circle apart.

3. Now attach the loose end of the bell wire to the other pole of the dry cell (closing the circuit) and place the nail so that it will attract and move each paper clip in turn. In this way you will create an electromagnetic circuit, which also exists in a motor. The cardboard disc will represent the moving part or rotor of the motor.

4. Try also to make the disc or rotor move with a permanent magnet instead of an electromagnetic force.

Showing Your Answers at the Science Fair

1. Fasten your dry cell and wire to a panel of wood or a heavy sheet of cardboard. Mount the pencil and paper disc close to the battery.

2. Place the permanent magnet close to the pencil and paper disc so that it may be used to move the disc.

3. Explain in writing how you think electricity makes a motor turn or spin.

New Questions

How can a stronger motor be made?

How could a stronger motor be adapted to move things?

What Do You Think?

Can static electricity be created in many materials?

Finding the Answer

1. Cut or tear some tiny strips of paper.

2. Find something made of plastic, such as a comb, as well as some things of glass, metal and (if possible) bone. Also collect some pieces of different materials, such as wool, cotton, silk, fur, nylon, etc.

3. Rub each of the hard materials, such as the comb, on each of the soft materials. After rubbing each one, try to move or pick up the strips of paper. Notice which combinations of hard and soft materials created the most electricity and which the least.

This static-electricity tester is easily made. The folded piece of paper shown here is balanced on the point of a pencil. Any static electricity in the comb will cause the paper to move around.

Showing Your Answers at the Science Fair

1. Attach all of your tested materials to a large sheet of cardboard. Arrange them first, of course, in the order in which they created the most static electricity. Number and name each one.
2. Make a static-electricity detector. Fold a stiff piece of paper and balance it on the point of a pencil. The pencil may be held upright in a spool or a lump of clay. When an object containing static electricity is brought near the detector the folded paper will move toward it.
3. Explain in writing what you have done and what you have learned about static electricity.

New Questions

Why are we able to create more static electricity in some materials than in others?

What reactions aside from static electricity does rubbing cause?

What Do You Think?

Can we learn to identify the clouds we see every day?

Finding the Answer

1. Look in encyclopedias and other reference books for pictures of cloud formations and their names. Investigate the significance of each of these formations.
2. Practice identifying the clouds you see on the way to and from school each day.
3. Practice drawing some outline pictures of basic cloud formations.
4. Try taking some snapshots of typical cloud formations.

Showing Your Answers at the Science Fair

1. Cut pictures of cloud formations from papers and magazines and mount them on a large sheet of cardboard or on paper in a folder.
2. Photograph cloud formations and mount the prints on cardboard. Give the names and dates of the photos, names of formations, their height and significance. Also state the film and camera used, as well as the lens openings and speeds if an adjustable camera is used.
3. Keep a daily cloud record for a week or two and show the related weather conditions. What general weather conditions preceded, accompanied and followed these formations? Give the temperatures, humidity and wind speeds.

New Questions

Can weather condictions be predicted from cloud formations alone?
How significant is the height of a cloud formation?

What Do You Think?

Why are coastal cities warmer in winter and cooler in summer than inland cities at the same latitude and elevation?

Finding the Answer

1. Fill two equal-size pots or pans, one with water and one with soil.

2. Allow both to stand indoors until they are at room temperature. Check this with two thermometers, one in each pot. Record the times and temperatures.
3. On a cold day place both pots outdoors (in the shade) and read both thermometers at five-minute intervals. Again record the times and temperatures on paper carefully.
4. After both containers are equally cold bring them indoors and read both thermometers again at five-minute intervals. Again record times and temperatures.
5. Place the readings in two columns, one for the container of soil and one for the container of water. Note which pot changed temperature faster.

Showing Your Answers at the Science Fair

1. Exhibit both pots and both thermometers.
2. Display your records of the temperature changes.
3. Explain step by step what you did and what you discovered. Tell how the soil and water in the pots are related to the temperatures of coastal and inland cities.

New Questions

How do ocean currents affect coastal temperature?
How do mountains affect temperature?

What Do You Think?

How does our climate compare with that of a city two hundred or more miles north or south of us?

Finding the Answer

1. Using geography books, almanacs and encyclopedias, discover the length of each season in two selected cities, yours and one two hundred miles north or south.
2. Compare the average temperatures of winters and summers in the cities.
3. Compare the amounts of rainfall and snow.
4. Compare the frequencies of storms and dry spells.
5. Compare the kinds of crops and vegetables grown.

Showing Your Answers at the Science Fair

1. Display a map and pinpoint the location of both cities. Show also on the map a postcard or magazine picture of each city.
2. Make a large chart which compares the climate of the two cities.
3. Show how differently the sun's rays strike the earth at the latitudes where the two cities are located.
4. Explain in writing exactly what you have done and what you have discovered about the climate of the two cities.

New Questions

What latitude has the most attractive climate for you?
Why do the sun's rays strike the earth differently at various latitudes?

What Do You Think?

How does one read a weather map?

Finding the Answer

1. Locate a weather map in a local newspaper.
2. Take the map to a library and consult reference works for a more complete explanation of the symbols.
3. Test your understanding by reading several other maps. Check with the local weather bureau or a science teacher to remove your remaining doubts about the symbols.

Showing Your Answers at the Science Fair

1. Exhibit two or more weather maps on a large cardboard chart which also gives the meaning of all the symbols used on the maps.
2. Make a large drawing which shows all the wind-speed symbols, fronts and cloud conditions. Illustrate this drawing with pictures of various weather conditions cut from newspapers and magazines.
3. Explain in writing everything you have done and what you have discovered.

New Questions
How often and from where does the national weather bureau get its information.

How can predictions be made on the basis of the reports to the weather bureau?

What Do You Think?
How are we affected by dust and smoke in the air?

Finding the Answer
1. Observe the amount of dust in the air which falls with and collects on the snow in the wintertime. Heat some snow in a container and strain the water through a clean white cloth. At other times, when there is no snow, tack a white cloth to a board to collect dust and smoke particles.
2. To measure the amount of dust that collects daily, tack a long piece of cotton batting to a board and cover the cotton with another board. Expose an equal amount of batting each day by pulling the cover board off the same amount each day.
3. Write to your nearest city air-pollution control body and ask for information concerning the amount and the nature of the polluting elements in your locality.
4. Ask your nearest city government for copies of city laws and regulations concerning air pollution.
5. Consult your local weather bureau and reference books about fog and smog.

Showing Your Answers at the Science Fair
1. Exhibit two charts, one showing the good and helpful effects of dust in the atmosphere and one showing the bad effects. Use newspaper and magazine pictures to illustrate clouds, fog, smog, and air-pollution sources.
2. Present a chart showing the many ways that dust and smoke get into the air.
3. Explain in writing all that you have done and what you have discovered.

New Questions
Why is it difficult to prevent air pollution?

How dangerous to people is air pollution?

What Do You Think?

How do large balloons differ from blimps and dirigibles?

Finding the Answer

1. Investigate lighter-than-air craft in reference books. Discover the differences in their shape and purpose. Learn how they are made to go up and down.
2. Discover how dirigibles are able to move forward and backward.
3. Experiment with a helium-filled balloon purchased in a ten-cent store or a public park. Build a gondola for it and see if it can be ballasted to float at a single height.
4. Write to the national weather bureau for information and pictures of weather balloons.

Showing Your Answers at the Science Fair

1. Exhibit photographs of balloons used in weather research. Also exhibit photos or drawings of dirigibles. Explain in writing how each is used and how they differ.
2. Prepare and show a chart of the altitudes and dates of balloon penetrations of the atmosphere. Explain why balloons are used instead of dirigibles.
3. Make a cardboard or balsa model of a famous balloon or dirigible. Explain how it functions.

New Questions

How does the weather bureau combine the use of radar with balloons?
How have balloons extended the use of television?

What Do You Think?

How does a jet engine work?

Finding the Answer

1. Construct a pair of jet-balloon toy racers. The first step is to inflate two long balloons and tie a short string to each end of both balloons. Fasten

97

paper clips to the free end of the short strings and slip the clips over a long piece of string or wire which is pulled tight between two chairs or wooden uprights. The strings at the open end or neck of the balloons should be tied around a small paper tube which can be pinched to hold the air in and let go to start the race.

2. Look in reference books to discover how a jet engine or a jet airplane works. Find out where rapid burning takes place and why the engine moves forward.

3. Discover how a jet engine differs from a rocket engine.

Showing Your Answers at the Science Fair

1. Exhibit your jet-balloon toy racer.

2. Mount pictures of jet airplanes and, if possible, a picture of a jet engine on a sheet of cardboard. These may be secured from aircraft companies and airlines.

3. Present a map of the United States on which you can draw the routes of jet aircraft, automobiles, and trains across the continent. Mark the time span each kind of transportation requires for this trip.

4. Explain in writing how a jet engine works and how they compare with piston engines and with rockets.

New Questions

Are jets taking the place of piston-type engines in airplanes?
Will rockets ever take the place of jet engines?

What Do You Think?

How can burning gasoline make a car move?

Finding the Answer

1. Investigate to discover in what part of an engine gasoline is burned. Look in reference books; ask a garage mechanic; ask your parents if they have an auto manual. Ask any interested adult who might know to explain how burning gasoline makes the wheels of a car turn.

2. Discover the meaning and function of these engine parts: the cylinder, the piston, connecting rod, crankshaft and driveshaft. Build a cardboard model of a cylinder with piston and connecting rod.

Showing Your Answers at the Science Fair

1. Exhibit your cardboard model of a cylinder.
2. Show a model airplane engine if one is available. Indicate the names of the parts.
3. Exhibit drawings or cutaway views of a motor boat, motorcycle or airplane engine.
4. Explain in writing exactly how burning gasoline moves a car. Tell also what else you have learned about gasoline engines.

New Questions

Is burning gasoline more efficient than using steam?
Is burning gasoline more efficient than burning oil?

What Do You Think?

What keeps an airplane in the air?

Finding the Answer

1. Observe what keeps a kite in the air and on what kind of days a kite flies best.
2. Cut a long strip of paper (1" x 8") and blow over the top of it (not underneath). Find out why the paper rises as you blow over it.
3. Carve a model-airplane propeller or buy one and pull a string or wire through the shaft hole. Holding the string or wire taut, spin the propeller with a sharp blow of the hand. Observe the direction in which the propeller moves.
4. Investigate the meaning of the words "lift" and "thrust." Discover how lift is created. Consult aircraft manuals and other reference books for this information.

Have someone help you fly a kite so you can feel the wind pulling on the cord in your hands. Could this "pulling" be used to put the wind to work? What is a good kite-flying day like? Would these also be good days for the work of a windmill?

Showing Your Answers at the Science Fair

1. Mount your propeller on a panel of cardboard or wood along with a section of a model wing. Indicate with crayon or ink where the kite and vacuum effects occur. Indicate how a propeller works.
2. Show how a jet engine pushes a plane forward in the same way that a balloon is pushed forward by the air inside the balloon.
3. Explain in writing what you have done and what you have discovered.

New Questions

Why can't airplanes fly into outer space?
Why can't balloons travel to the moon?

What Do You Think?

How is the direction of an airplane controlled in flight?

Finding the Answer

1. Look in reference books for the names and locations of "control surfaces."

2. Construct a light cardboard glider with control surfaces. Adjust the control surfaces to change flight direction. Color each control surface for easy identification.
3. Construct a model airplane or glider with control surfaces and fly it outdoors. Practice changing control surfaces to change direction of flight.

Showing Your Answers at the Science Fair

1. Mount your model airplane or glider on a large panel.
2. Indicate the location of control surfaces and how they work.
3. Exhibit a chart showing the positions of each control surface for a "right bank," a "left bank" and for gaining and losing altitude.
4. Explain in writing all you have done and what you have learned.

New Questions

What instrument tells the pilot how far his plane is from the ground?
How do bank and turn indicators work?

What Do You Think?

Why are rockets used for space flights?

Finding the Answer

1. Investigate to discover how much oxygen there is in the air at various distances from the earth.
2. Compare rockets with jet engines. Why couldn't jet engines be used in space flights?
3. Construct cardboard or balsa models of one or more famous rockets. Show the location of fuel and oxygen tanks, also the pump and combustion chamber.
4. Consult encyclopedias and science books for pictures and information on rockets. See the periodicals in your own public library.

Showing Your Answers at the Science Fair

1. Display your cardboard or balsa models and explain how a rocket engine works.

This Delta rocket is being used to launch an S-3a spacecraft. It will help our scientists learn more about space weather. The spacecraft is at the top; the rocket or launch vehicle is partly covered by clouds.

2. Exhibit a large drawing which compares a jet engine and a rocket engine. Indicate the differences.
3. Explain everything you have done and what you have learned.

New Questions

Why do we want to investigate outer space?
How powerful are the rockets now being built?

What Do You Think?

Why are multistage rockets used to launch satellites?

Finding the Answer

1. Investigate the meaning of the word "weight." Compare the gravitational pull of the earth with that of other planets. This information can be found in astronomy and other science books.
2. Find the weight of a rocket and its space capsule. Learn exactly how its weight decreases as it moves away from the earth.
3. Discover how many tons of fuel must be used to lift a one-ton satellite off the ground.

Showing Your Answers at the Science Fair

1. Exhibit a cardboard or wooden model you have designed of a two- or three-stage rocket. Show where these stages are connected and at what point in their trajectory they might separate.
2. Draw a picture of the possible trajectory of such a rocket and indicate where the stages might separate.
3. Explain the lessening effect of gravity and why such a great force is needed to "blast off" from the earth.
4. Explain what you now know about multistage rockets.

New Questions

Does the earth's gravitational pull actually end somewhere in outer space?
How does the sun's gravity affect us?

This artist's version of the Delta launch vehicle and S-3 spacecraft shows some of the inside parts. This is a three-stage rocket which is nine stories high and weighs 57 tons. The payload will orbit at 19,000 miles per hour.

What Do You Think?

Can any of our planets be seen with the naked eye?

Finding the Answer

1. Consult your local newspapers to see if they give information about planets which are visible to the naked eye. If so, find out the last time any planet was visible.
2. Look in such publications as *Natural History,* a publication of the Museum of Natural History in New York City. Also look for the *Science Newsletter* in your local library. These periodicals often carry such information.
3. Locate the observatory nearest your home and write to it for information about planets which may soon be visible to the naked eye. Some astronomy books also carry this kind of information.

4. Following the information given by these authorities, look for a given planet in the sky. Ask your friends to help you sight the planet. Record the time, date and location of the planet. Record also the names of the people who sighted the planet with you.

Showing Your Answers at the Science Fair

1. Draw a picture of the planet you have observed and show its general position in the sky. Give the related information about size, distance and orbit of the planet.
2. Explain how to locate such a planet in the sky so that others may view one.
3. Explain in writing what you have done and what you now know about viewing planets.

New Questions

Do planets give off their own light?

Why can some planets never be seen with the naked eye?

What Do You Think?

In what ways does the shape of the moon seem to change?

Finding the Answer

1. On a large sheet of paper draw a blank calendar with enough squares to equal the days of the coming month.
2. Each night of that month that the moon is visible draw its shape in the proper square. If clouds obscure the moon, draw a cloud in the square.
3. Underneath the calendar, or on a separate sheet of paper, make a list of the nights on which you saw a full moon, a half moon and a quarter moon.
4. Consult astronomy and general reference books for the reasons the moon appears to change shape.

Showing Your Answers at the Science Fair

1. Mount your calendar and your list on a large sheet of cardboard. Use crayons or paints to color it for display.

2. Explain in writing the ways in which the moon seems to change shape and why.

New Questions

Why does the moon appear white on some nights and yellow on others?
Does the moon really change shape?

What Do You Think?

What causes the moon to give off light?

Finding the Answer

1. Hold a small flashlight or a candle so that it lights a ball or a balloon in a dark room. Have a friend hold the light while you walk around the ball or balloon. Notice how, in certain places as you walk, the ball seems only partly lighted.
2. Look in an encyclopedia or a book on astronomy for pictures which show the sun, the earth and the moon. Discover the source of the light which comes from the moon.

Showing Your Answers at the Science Fair

1. On a large sheet of heavy cardboard cement a tennis ball or a small rubber ball. At a suitable distance from it attach, with wire or string, a small pen or pocket flashlight. With the small light turned on, darken that part of the ball which is not lighted by the pen.
2. Mark or label the ball "moon" and the penlight "sun." If the ball is half lighted by the penlight, mark the word "half-moon" under the ball.
3. Present in writing what you now know about the source of the light which comes from the moon.

New Questions

Why does the moon seem brighter on some nights than on others?
Can the moon be seen during the day?

What Do You Think?

Is the expression, "What goes up must come down," still a true one?

Finding the Answer

1. Consult books and periodicals in your library dealing with space exploration to discover if there are rockets and capsules which have not returned to the earth. Find out what has happened to vehicles sent to probe the moon, Mars and Venus.
2. In view of the fact that the earth is ball-like and turning in space and that people live on all parts of it, what is the meaning of the words "up" and "down."

Showing Your Answers at the Science Fair

1. Show pictures of capsules and rocket sections which have not returned to the earth. Secure these from newspapers and magazines or by writing to the National Aeronautics and Space Administration in Washington, D.C.
2. Draw a large circle to represent the earth and use arrows to show that things near the earth are drawn toward the earth's center. Indicate the gravitational force of the earth, the moon and the sun.
3. Present in writing the real meaning of the expression "What goes up must come down."

New Questions

How far out in space does the earth's gravity extend?

Would an astronaut who may someday land on the moon theoretically appear to be rightside up or upside down when viewed from earth?

What Do You Think?

What causes a satellite to stay in orbit?

Finding the Answer

1. Experiment with a ball on a string. What part do you think velocity plays in causing the ball to orbit. Will the ball orbit without attaining a certain velocity?

Here is an S-3a energetic particle satellite as it would appear in orbit. What forces would keep this satellite in orbit around the earth?

2. Throw a ball over a house or some small building. What force causes the ball to curve downward and to complete its journey? What would happen if this force did not exist?
3. Look in reference books dealing with space exploration to discover the parts played by velocity and by gravity in causing a satellite to stay in orbit.

Showing Your Answers at the Science Fair

1. Mount some photos or magazine pictures of rockets and satellites on a large sheet of cardboard or paper.
2. Draw a picture of a ball being thrown over a building and explain with arrows and words the parts played by the "blast off," velocity, and the force of gravity.
3. Draw a picture of a ball being orbited on a string. Indicate the parts played by velocity and by gravity.
4. Explain everything you have done and what you have discovered in writing.

New Questions

Why are some orbits larger than others?
Why are orbits different in shape?

What Do You Think?

Why are mirrors such good reflectors of light?

Finding the Answer

1. Find out how mirrors are constructed. Scratch the back of one or two cheap mirrors with a piece of metal and see if you can detect what materials were used there.
2. Ask your local glazier for the names of companies which make mirrors. Write to them for any printed information they may have.
3. Look in reference books in your library for information about the construction and manufacture of mirrors.
4. Discover the difference between common glass and plate glass.

5. Place a piece of tin foil or aluminum foil back of a piece of glass. Does this make a good mirror? If not, why?

Showing Your Answers at the Science Fair

1. Mount on a large cardboard all of the materials you have examined. Include all the mirrors, glass and pieces of foil. Explain how each was used.
2. On one section of the cardboard draw a picture which shows the main parts and materials used on a good mirror. This should show the construction of the mirror.
3. Explain in writing why you think mirrors are such good reflectors of light. Explain also what you have done and what you have learned.

New Questions

Why are glass mirrors used more often than metal ones?
Why is a plate-glass mirror more expensive than others?

What Do You Think?

How much better do some common materials reflect light than others?

Finding the Answer

1. Construct a testing device using a milk carton, a flashlight, and a ruler. Stick a small pen-light through one end of a carton. At the opposite end of the carton cut a rectangular opening in one of the sides. Underneath the opening, on the sides of the box cut slots at a 45-degree angle. Into these slots slide the materials you wish to test. Try colored papers, metal foils, glass, cloth, wood, etc.
2. As each piece of material rests in the 45-degree slot, turn on the pen-light and hold a sheet of white paper over the hole in the top side of the carton to find the height at which the reflected light disappears from the paper. The distance each material will reflect light onto the white paper can be measured with a ruler taped to the carton.
3. Keep records on each material tested. Write a detailed description of each material and the distance it reflects light.

Showing Your Answers at the Science Fair

1. Exhibit your testing device and the materials you have tested.
2. Display a chart showing how each of the materials reflected light.
3. Present in writing the procedure you followed in testing these materials and your explanation of how much better some of these materials reflected light than others.

New Questions

Why does color affect the ability to reflect light?
Why does smoothness and texture affect the ability to reflect light?

What Do You Think?

How can mirrors be used as toys?

Finding the Answer

1. Make a simple periscope. Fold a large piece of cardboard into a square pipe and tape it together. Cut a hole in the front top of the pipe and in the back at the bottom. Insert a mirror on a 45-degree angle in the pipe in front of each hole. Small ten-cent store mirrors measuring at least two by four inches will do for this purpose.
2. With pieces of tinplate or metal mirrors, make some crazy mirrors by bending them in various directions. These may be fastened to a piece of wood with tacks and tape.
3. Make some model highways by drawing on cardboard. Use mirrors stuck in clay to guide toy cars around sharp curves and over hills.
4. Produce some reversed writing and read it with a mirror. Do this by placing a piece of plain paper over a piece of carbon paper with the carbon side up. Have a friend write something on the plain paper and then turn it over before handing it to you. Read this reversed writing by holding it in front of a mirror.
5. "Making money" with mirrors: Hinge two small mirrors together along one edge with tape. Stand them on edge with the mirrors forming a right angle. Place a coin on the table between the mirrors and see how many coin images are formed. See if you can increase the number by changing the angles of the mirrors. Substitute a lighted candle for the coin.

A periscope can easily be made from a large sheet of cardboard and two small mirrors. Notice the forty-five-degree angles of the two mirrors. The bottom one is partly hidden under Joseph Vitolo's right hand.

Showing Your Answers at the Science Fair

1. Exhibit your toys and toy materials. Explain how each works.
2. Explain in writing the laws of reflection. These are available in many reference books.

New Questions

What kinds of materials and surfaces serve as natural mirrors?
When and where were the first mirrors made and used?

What Do You Think?

How are rocks formed?

Finding the Answer

1. Investigate to discover the meaning of the words "igneous," "sedimentary," "metamorphic." Consult reference books in your library and visit a museum, if possible. A friend who is a "rock hound" may be of some help.
2. Collect samples of the three basic kinds of rocks mentioned above and

112

start your own collection. Check the identity of these rocks with pictures in reference books or at a museum in your locality.

3. Discover what kinds of rocks are typical of your neighborhood.

Showing Your Answers at the Science Fair

1. Exhibit some of the rocks found in your own neighborhood and explain how they were probably formed.
2. Display your entire collection of rocks and indicate the process by which each was probably formed. Number and name the rocks.
3. Present in writing your own explanation of how rocks are formed.

New Questions

How are the ages of rocks determined?
How old are the oldest rocks known?

What Do You Think?

In how many ways are rocks useful?

Finding the Answer

1. Find the meaning of the word "rock." Use more than one reference book for information about rocks.
2. Discover the meaning of these words:
   a. marble,
   b. granite,
   c. sandstone,
   d. shale,
   e. slate,
   f. limestone,
   g. terrazzo.

   See if you can locate samples of these in your own neighborhood.
3. Collect as many samples of these kinds of rocks as possible.

Showing Your Answers at the Science Fair

1. Display your collection of rocks. Place them in boxes or cement them to heavy cardboard. Number and name as many as you can.

2. Make up a large display card showing pictures and drawings of rocks in use. This can include houses, porches, patios, fireplaces, chimneys, etc.

New Questions

How are rocks formed?
Are all rocks hard?

What Do You Think?

Where does rainwater go?

Finding the Answer

1. Secure two glass jars of equal size. In the bottom of one place a few rocks, then pebbles, then sand, and add some soil on top. Pour a cup of water into both jars and allow them to set outside in the sun. Look at both jars twice a day until the water has disappeared from both. Note which jar held water, or moisture, longer. Where did the water go? Find the meaning of the word "evaporation."
2. Pour a cup of water into each of three glasses. Place a few leaves over the top of one glass. Squirt a few drops of oil into another one. Put all three glasses into the sun and keep a record of the exact time it takes for the water to evaporate from all three glasses.
3. Examine the roots of two or three small potted plants. Notice how the roots have grown into the damp earth. Ask some adults who know something about plants if the plants take much water out of the soil.
4. Figure out how much water your pets drink in a week or a month.

Showing Your Answers at the Science Fair

1. Exhibit your glass jars and a written explanation of how the soil absorbs and holds water.
2. Show your glasses of water along with the leaves and oil. Explain in writing how water evaporates from puddles, lakes, and rivers, and how some things, such as leaves and oil, slow evaporation.
3. Display a potted plant and explain how all plants use water. Also, explain how people and other animals, including pets, use water.

New Questions

Of what is water made?

What happens to evaporated water?

What Do You Think?

Where does the motion in motion pictures come from?

Finding the Answer

1. Buy a small, pocket-size notebook, or make one with a scissors and stapler. Draw a small arrow and a small target on the edges of all the sheets, but on each succeeding sheet draw the arrow a bit closer to the target. Have the arrow hit the target on the last few sheets. Then, thumb the edges of the sheets quickly and notice how at certain speeds the arrow seems to be in motion.

2. Placing an animal in a cage in motion: Cut a three-by-five index card in half with a pair of scissors. Draw a bird on one side of the card and a cage on the other. Slit the eraser on the end of a new pencil so that it will hold the card upright. Now spin the pencil between the palms of your hands. Notice that at certain speeds the bird seems to fly inside the cage.

3. Ask someone who has a movie camera for a short length of exposed and unwanted film strip. Notice the small differences in adjoining pictures. Also inquire as to the speeds at which a projector moves the film.

Showing Your Answers at the Science Fair

1. Exhibit your notebook with arrows and targets, your bird-in-a-cage device, and the length of movie film. Mount these on a sheet of cardboard and explain how they are used to produce the effect of motion.

2. Explain slow motion, normal and fast motion. Tell in writing how the camera's shutter action is related to projector speeds.

New Questions

How can the use of a slow-motion and a fast-action camera be detected?

How can fast shutter action be detected when there is fast projector motion?

What Do You Think?

How can the developing of film and the printing of pictures be done at home?

Finding the Answer

1. Buy an inexpensive kit for developing film and printing pictures. The necessary items can also be purchased separately. They include: a tank for developing the negative, three pans for printing, a safelight, contact paper and chemicals.
2. Follow the instructions given in your kit or those given in many photography magazines and books.
3. Your darkroom must be located near running water. This might be in a basement, bathroom or kitchen.
4. Carry through the complete process yourself. Take some pictures, develop the film and print the pictures.

Showing Your Answers at the Science Fair

1. Display the equipment you have used to develop and print.
2. Name each piece of equipment and describe what it will do.
3. Show some samples of your own work.
4. Explain in writing all you have done and what you have learned.

New Questions

What conditions are necessary for a good darkroom?
What are the qualities of a good print?
What is the composition of the chemicals used in developing and printing?

What Do You Think?

How does a box camera work?

Finding the Answer

1. Notice where the light reflected from an object enters a camera and forms an image on the film. Construct a pinhole viewer from a salt or cereal box. Do this by punching a pinhole in one end of the box and covering the other end, which has been removed, with wax paper. The

This pinhole viewer has a piece of wax paper stretched over the end of the salt box. A tiny pinhole is centered in the other end. How is this device like a camera? In what ways is it different?

paper can be held with a rubber band. Point the pinhole toward a bright or well-lighted object. Notice the position of the image on the wax paper.

2. Remove the back of a box camera and cover the opening with wax paper. Set the shutter to "Time" and open the aperture to the largest f stop. Point the camera at some well-lighted objects. Notice the position of the image on the wax paper. Change the size of the opening or the f stop and view the image again.

3. Use a magnifying glass to view various sizes of prints and pictures. Measure the distance at which the glass produces a sharp image. Notice how the glass brings the image into focus as does a camera lens.

Showing Your Answers at the Science Fair

1. Display your pinhole viewer and explain the purpose of the pinhole and the wax paper.

2. Exhibit a box camera with wax paper taped over the open back. Explain how the lens and shutter work to control the amount of light.

3. Make a large crayon drawing of a box camera. Explain how it works.

4. Secure some diagrams and pictures from booklets and brochures. Mount these, showing camera parts and indicating their functions.

New Questions

What is a prefocused lens?

How is a twin-lens reflex camera different from an ordinary box camera?

117

What Do You Think?

How does film preserve an image?

Finding the Answer

1. Buy a few sheets of contact paper from a photo store. Secure a small piece of glass and a few small, flat objects, such as keys and coins. Locate a few old snapshot negatives too.
2. Place a sheet of contact paper on a flat surface with the emulsion side up (the emulsion side is the shiny one). Now place a key or some coins on top of the paper and expose it to the sun until the paper darkens. Remove the key or coins and notice how the sunlight changes the uncovered parts of the paper.
3. This time place a negative over the contact paper and the piece of glass over the negative. Expose this to the sunlight. Experiment to find the exposure time which produces the best picture.
4. From your local photography store or a film company secure a pamphlet which tells you in detail how to develop negatives and print from them. Ask for information too about the chemicals used on negatives and on papers.

Showing Your Answers at the Science Fair

1. Arrange for display on a large sheet of cardboard all of the materials you have experimented with. Include an empty film box, a roll of film, contact paper, negatives, etc.
2. Exhibit your own negatives and prints.
3. Explain how film preserves an image and how prints are made. Present in writing everything you have done to learn how an image is preserved on film.

New Questions

Are the emulsions on developing papers and film stock made of the same chemicals?

Are the emulsions on all developing papers the same?

PROJECTS FOR THE SIXTH, SEVENTH AND EIGHTH GRADES

What Do You Think?

How far is my home from school?

Finding the Answer

1. Estimate or guess the distance and record it in your notebook.
2. If possible, check a street map containing a scale of miles. Record the distance between home and school figured from the map.
3. Practice walking with one-yard strides (measured from the middle of one foot to the middle of the other) and then count the number of such strides between your home and school. After figuring the distance in miles or fractions thereof, record this distance with the others.
4. Ask some adults who have checked this distance on the meter in their car. Record this measurement along with the others.
5. Measure off fifty or one hundred yards and trot that distance while someone times you with a watch. Then, if possible, trot all the way to school at the same speed. From the time it takes, figure the distance and record this with the other figures.
6. Construct a measuring wheel. Cut a circle out of Masonite or plywood of slightly less than than $11\frac{1}{2}$-inch diameter ($\frac{1}{32}$-inch less). This will

119

This close-up of a measuring wheel shows the Masonite wheel, the slot which was sawed to hold the wheel, and the strap-iron clicker which enables the user to hear each revolution of the three-foot wheel.

give you a circle the circumference of which is approximately 36 inches or three feet. Cut a slot in a stick which is long enough to serve as a handle and is at least 2 inches wide. The slot should be a trifle wider than the thickness of the Masonite disc. Use a machine screw and a nut to hold the disc in the slot and to serve as an axle. Another screw fastened near the edge of the disc will serve to make a clicking sound when a piece of scrap iron attached to the handle hits it once during each revolution of the disc. Each revolution of the wheel, of course, measures off one yard on the ground. With this wheel measure the distance to school and record the measurement.

Showing Your Answers at the Science Fair

1. Exhibit a chart which shows all of the measurements and estimates you have made.
2. Display your measuring wheel, map and drawings of the other methods used.
3. State in writing which one you think was the most accurate method and also tell the weaknesses of each.

New Questions

What more accurate methods and tools might have been used?
Can all errors be eliminated in measurement?

What Do You Think?

How do thermometers work?

Finding the Answer

1. Construct a water-bottle thermometer. Fill a small bottle with colored water and then cork it tightly. Use a cork through which you have inserted a glass tube or a soda straw. Allow the water in the bottle to adjust to room temperature and then mark the level of the water on the straw or tube. Next place the bottle in the sunlight for several hours and then mark the level of the water. Finally, hold the bottle in cold water and note how far the water in the straw will drop.

2. Investigate to discover why mercury is most often used in thermometers. Discover also what other substances are used instead of mercury. Inquire about the basic changes that take place in liquids and other materials in response to temperature changes.

Showing Your Answers at the Science Fair

1. Display your water bottle thermometer and indicate how one is constructed.
2. Exhibit a large card on which you have indicated the results of the various tests conducted with the thermometer.
3. Present in writing the procedure you followed and indicate the reasons various substances are used in thermometers.

New Questions

What are the causes of temperature changes in the human body?
Why is the Fahrenheit thermometer used in some places and the centigrade in others?

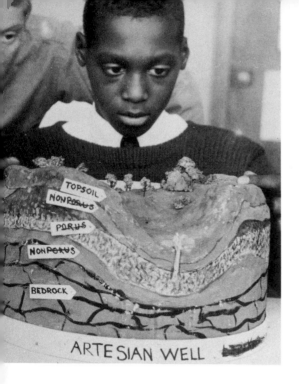

Labels on model: TOPSOIL, NONPOROUS, POROUS, NONPOROUS, BEDROCK

ARTESIAN WELL

This project shows the rock structure which permits artesian wells. Why do artesian wells often flow naturally? Why must the water from some artesian wells be pumped out?

What Do You Think?

Why do artesian wells flow naturally?

Finding the Answer

1. If possible, visit the location of an artesian well. Note the topography of the surrounding terrain. Note if a pump is or has been used.
2. Investigate the meaning of such terms as "impermeable strata" and "permeable strata." Visit any local museum which might have earth-science displays and consult reference books for information.

Showing Your Answers at the Science Fair

1. Build a papier-mâché and plaster model which shows the rock structure and strata necessary for an artesian well. Show the location of the well and the surface topography. Use paint to color the various strata and other parts of the model. Name each part and indicate its function.
2. Present in writing everything you have done and your answer to the question of why artesian wells flow naturally.

New Questions

Is the flow of an artesian well constant and permanent?
What kinds of pumps are used in wells?

What Do You Think?

What is the basic composition of water?

Finding the Answer

1. Investigate the meaning of the words "molecule" and "atom." Use school texts and other reference books for research.
2. Locate some diagrams showing the composition of a molecule of water.
3. Learn what happens to the hydrogen and oxygen components when water is heated.

Showing Your Answers at the Science Fair

1. Use corks and dowel rods or Tinker Toy parts to show the various parts of a molecule of water. Paint the corks which represent oxygen one color

These round corks and thin dowel rods were used to show the composition of a molecule of water (H_2O). The yellow ball in the center is the nucleus of the oxygen atom. The hydrogen atoms are on the right and left.

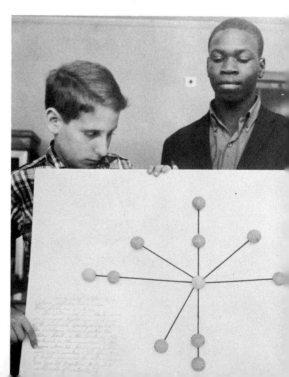

and the hydrogen parts another. Also show the nuclei of the oxygen atoms. Mount this assembly on a large sheet of cardboard with cement or wire.

2. Explain in writing the steps you have followed and what you have discovered about the composition of water.

New Questions

What is meant by the phrase "atomic energy"?
What is "atomic weight"?

What Do You Think?

How can we measúre the altitude of stars and planets?

Finding the Answer

1. Consult astronomy books and other reference materials in the library to discover what instruments are and have been used to measure the altitude and bearing of stars from the N.S. meridian.

With this astrolabe you can find the latitude and bearing of a star from the N.S. meridian. Of course it can be easily used to find the angular altitude of a star or any other object. It may also be called a theodolite.

2. Build a simple astrolabe or theodolite by securing three inexpensive metal protractors, a soda straw, a ¾″ x 1″ x 8″ stick of wood for an upright. A base piece will also be needed. This can measure approximately 6″ x 6″. A nut or a washer hanging to the end of the string on the upright will enable you to hold the instrument parallel to the horizon line. A scrap-metal pointer attached to the bottom end of the upright will enable you to measure horizontal angles. Attach the two protractors to the base and one to the upright as shown in the accompanying picture.

Showing Your Answers at the Science Fair

1. Display your astrolabe and explain how it works.
2. Display a brief paper you have written on the history and use of the astrolabe and the theodolite.

New Questions

Why has it been important to measure the angular altitude of the stars?
How is a sextant like an astrolabe?

What Do You Think?

How can we measure the amount of moisture in the air?

Finding the Answer

1. Construct a hair hygrometer. Use a small piece of wood and a length of human hair which has been washed in Carbona and dried. Cement or tape one end of the hair to the top of the board and the other end to a paper arrow at the bottom. As the hair absorbs moisture it will contract and move the arrow upwards, and as it dries the hair will lengthen and allow the arrow to drop.
2. Check variations in humidity every day for several days. Check indoors and outdoors.
3. Keep a calendar chart and record each day's observations.
4. Compare your observations with those of the weather bureau.

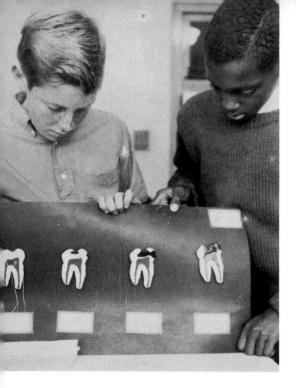

Harvey and Jo are shown here with a series of plaster models which show the development of dental caries. The plaster models were painted with three colors: red, white and black. They are attached with wire.

Showing Your Answers at the Science Fair

1. Exhibit your hair hygrometer and explain how it works.
2. Display your calendar chart with the recorded observations.
3. Explain in writing all you have done and what you have learned.

New Questions

Does an increase in humidity always mean rain?
What causes changes in humidity?

What Do You Think?

What are the causes of cavities in our teeth?

Finding the Answer

1. In a reference book locate a picture which shows the structure of human teeth. Learn the names of the main parts of a tooth. Look up the word "caries" in the dictionary.
2. Discover how fermentation affects enamel.

Jo Chavis is pointing out a part of a villi. These are tiny, finger-like projections which line the walls of the small intestine. The villi aid in the absorption of food. This is an enlarged plaster cast. (See page 128)

3. Find the effects of putrefaction on dentine.
4. Check with your own dentist on the causes of cavities.

Showing Your Answers at the Science Fair

1. Make a series of plaster replicas of human teeth. Color the pulpal areas red. Show where the enamel ends and the dentine begins. Indicate the main parts of the tooth. On one replica show where fermentation might begin and on the others indicate its progress toward dentine destruction.
2. Explain in writing exactly what you have done to investigate the causes of cavities and what you have discovered.

New Questions

In what other ways can teeth be damaged?
What is the effect of fluorine on the enamel?

What Do You Think?

What parts of the human body enable foods to be absorbed into the bloodstream and how is this done?

Finding the Answer

1. Investigate the role of the villi. Discover the function of capillaries, veins, arteries and lacteal. Consult biology and other reference books for this information.
2. Ask your family doctor, if possible, how this absorption takes place and what factors might interfere.
3. Check the accuracy of your information with your science teacher.

Showing Your Answers at the Science Fair

1. Make an enlarged replica of one or more villus from plaster of Paris or clay. Mount this on a wood panel with wires.
2. Color the main parts of the villi with paint so that they can be easily identified. Name each part.
3. Present in writing how you think food is absorbed into the bloodstream and any related information which would help explain the process.

New Questions

How does food move in the intestine?
Does food absorption take place anywhere else in the body?

What Do You Think?

What is the real size and appearance of the human brain?

Finding the Answer

1. If possible, visit a museum where the brain and other parts of the body are exhibited.
2. Consult biology texts and general reference books for pictures and drawings of the human brain.
3. Discover the size range of the human brain and its relative weight.

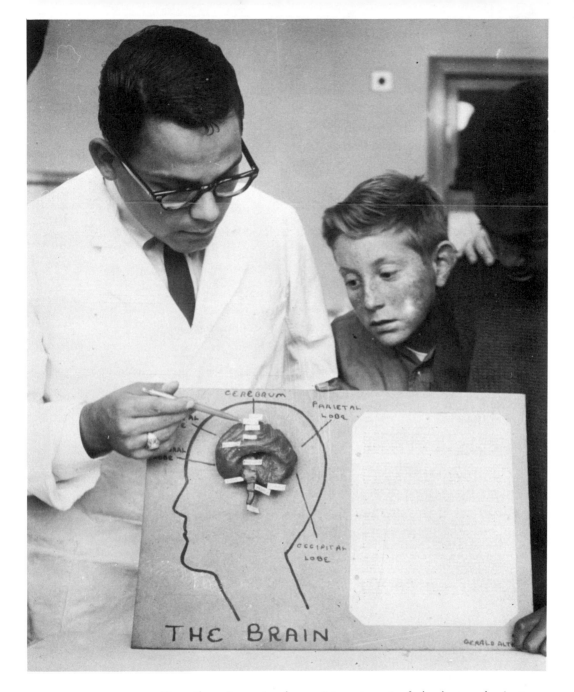

Here the science teacher points out part of the human brain to a science-fair participant, Harvey Brandwein. This is a clay model which Gerald Altman tried to make as accurate in size and shape as possible.

Showing Your Answers at the Science Fair

1. Paint one side of a 12″ x 18″ sheet of ¼-inch plywood or Masonite. Then draw on the painted side with ink or paint an outline or profile of the human head. Make this life-size.
2. Mold a clay model of the brain including as many detailed characteristics as possible. Embed a small stick of wood in the clay and some lightweight wires which can be used to attach the model to the panel.
3. Indicate on small white cards pinned to the model the various parts of the brain.
4. Explain in writing all you have done and what you have learned about the size and appearance of the brain.

New Questions

Does man have the largest brain of any animal?

How does a man's brain compare in size with that of a monkey, a gorilla and a chimpanzee?

What do ants do underground? This jar with a screw-top lid will make a good house for a colony of ants. Notice the nail which will hang in the lid and provide an opening to supply them with food and water.

What Do You Think?
What do ants do underground?

Finding the Answer
1. Use a large jar with a screw top for an ant house. Fill it with earth, sand and loam from the same area where the ants are found. After finding an anthill, dig beneath it deeply with a shovel. Scatter the contents of the shovel on a large sheet of paper. Look for a large queen ant, some eggs and many ordinary ants.
2. Place the queen, some eggs and other ants in the jar. Drive a large common nail through the lid of the jar and use the nail as a stopper. The nailhole can serve as an opening through which the ants may be fed with a drop of honey or sugar and water occasionally.
3. Wrap a black cloth around the jar so that the ants will work and live near the glass sides and not in the center of the jar.
4. Occasionally remove the cloth cover and observe what the ants are doing. Record their activities in a notebook. Include the times and dates of observations

Showing Your Answers at the Science Fair
1. Exhibit your ant house and indicate how it was filled and used.
2. Make a large chart which gives the dates, times and nature of the ant activity.
3. Explain in writing what you have done and what you have discovered.

New Questions
Do ants have brains?
Can the behavior of ants be changed?

What Do You Think?
To what extent can the behavior of white rats be modified?

Finding the Answer
1. Construct a simple maze and teach white rats to obtain food by following certain paths. Use box wood and epoxy cement to construct the maze.

Draw the location of the maze walls on a sheet of plywood first. Plans for a maze can be found in many science and general reference books. Cover the top with wire screening.

2. Place food containers in opposite sides of the maze and record how long it takes the rats to learn the new location.
3. Try water as a substitute for food.
4. Try some raw potato as a reward.

Showing Your Answers at the Science Fair

1. Display your maze with instructions on how to build one.
2. Exhibit a chart showing the number of trials and times it took the rats to locate the reward. Indicate the number and percentages of successful trials as compared to failures.
3. Present in writing everything you have done and what you think about the modifiability of rat behavior.

New Questions

How can a dog's behavior be modified?
Can a cat's behavior be modified?

What Do You Think?

How quickly do earthworms learn direction?

Finding the Answer

1. Construct a T-shaped maze of clear, flexible plastic, such as that found in scrapbooks or photo binders. Cut the plastic with scissors and then Scotch tape the pieces together to form a hollow letter T. Leave the bottom of the letter open.
2. Place some humus in one arm of the T and some vinegar-saturated cloth in the opposite arm.
3. Start the worm at the bottom of the T and see if he avoids the vinegar. Do this about one hundred times and record exactly what he does on each trial.

4. Place a piece of sandpaper in one arm of the T. Run the bare wire from a dry-cell battery to the sandpaper so that when the worm crawls over the sandpaper it will connect the two wires and complete the circuit. Start the worm in the bottom of the T and record how many times it moves over the wires. After a hundred trials disconnect the battery and see if the worm avoids the sandpaper.

Showing Your Answers at the Science Fair

1. Display your maze and all other equipment used. Indicate the methods of construction.
2. Exhibit a chart which shows the number of trials in each experiment and the results observed.
3. Explain in writing exactly how you have proceeded and what you have learned.

New Questions

Will other worms react in the same manner?
Do earthworms have a brain and a nervous system?

What Do You Think?

How much can tools and instruments aid our senses?

Finding the Answer

1. Collect several balls and ball-like objects. Have at least six objects.
2. Arrange all of these objects on a table and ask someone to estimate the weight of each of the objects without touching them. Do this with about five different people. Record each estimate carefully.
3. Repeat this with the same five people (if possible), except that this time they may be allowed to touch and pick up the objects before estimating their weight. Record these estimates.
4. Now weigh each of the objects on a scale, preferably a balance-type, and record their weight.
5. Fill a pan with water and ask several people to dip out, with an odd-size jar, exactly one cup of water. Measure and record the amount each person dips. Use a graduated measure for accurate results.

133

Here are several objects of varying size. Will your sense of sight tell you if the tennis ball weighs more than the marble, for example? Will your sense of touch give you an accurate answer to this question?

6. Fill a deep pan with cold water and have several people stick one hand into the water and estimate the temperature. Record each person's estimate and the real temperature of the water measured with a thermometer immediately afterward.
7. Have a number of people hold a ball of string in one hand and a pair of scissors in the other. Tell them to cut off one foot of string. Measure each piece cut off and record its true length.

Showing Your Answers at the Science Fair

1. Either exhibit the materials and equipment you have used or make a large drawing of them and indicate how they were used.
2. Explain in writing how tools and materials help our senses and enable us to make better judgments.

New Questions

Might the results be different if, for example, one thousand people were tested?

What would life be like without measuring tools to extend our senses?

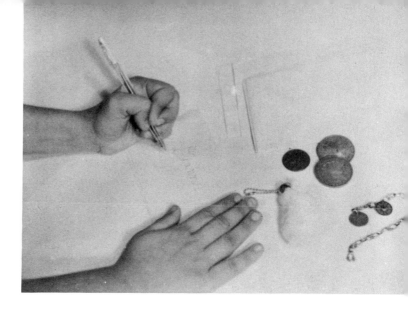

Has a lucky coin or a rabbit's foot ever brought you good luck? Can you explain "good luck" in such a way that most people would agree with you? If you have a lucky coin or charm you can try this project.

What Do You Think?

Is it helpful to carry a lucky coin or a rabbit's foot?

Finding the Answer

1. Place a "lucky" coin in one sealed envelope. Place another coin of a similar size in another envelope of the same size and kind. Using several ordinary coins of the same size in identical envelopes will improve the test.
2. Give each envelope to a different person to carry for a one day or a one-week period. Do not tell them the contents of the envelope, but keep track of who received the "lucky" coin.
3. At the end of the period ask each person if he has experienced exceptional luck or good fortune during the period. Record his answer in a notebook. Note which person carried the "lucky" coin.
4. List the responses. How many and which ones experienced exceptional luck? How many had no unusual experiences?

Note: This is, of course, what is called an uncontrolled experiment because the results will be determined not by the experiment alone but partly by people's feelings about a lucky coin and what constitutes luck.

135

Showing Your Answers at the Science Fair

1. Exhibit your coins and envelopes at the science fair.
2. Make a chart showing the number of people who participated and what responses resulted.
3. Explain in writing what results you think you discovered and why the results may be interesting but not conclusive or valid.

New Questions

May a superstition be partly truthful?

Why is the scientific method a more reliable guide to understanding the world than superstition?

PROJECTS FOR THE SEVENTH, EIGHTH AND NINTH GRADES

What Do You Think?

How can we measure the height of any tree or building?

Finding the Answer

1. Construct this simple measuring device. To the straight edge of a 180-degree protractor, tape a ruler or soda straw. With tape or cement attach one end of a string to the exact middle point of the straight edge of the protractor. At the other end of the string tie a small washer or fishing sinker.

2. Holding the protractor in one hand, sight along the straw or ruler until it is pointed exactly at the top of a building or tree. Now see where the weighted string hangs and crosses the arc of the protractor. If it is not at the 45-degree mark, move forward or backward, still sighting at the top of the tree or building, until the string crosses exactly at this mark.

3. At this point measure the distance on the ground to the building or tree from where you are standing. Add to this measurement the exact height of your eyes from the ground and this will give you the height of the building or tree.

4. Consult a geometry text or a teacher of mathematics to discover why this is a workable method of measuring height. Discover the many ways triangles are used in measurement.

5. Check the accuracy of your methods by measuring a few known heights. Finally, measure a number of unknown heights.

Showing Your Answers at the Science Fair

1. Exhibit your measuring device attached to a large sheet of cardboard.
2. Also draw a tree or some other object to be measured on the cardboard. Indicate with lines and arrows how the measurement is made.

New Questions

Why isn't this method an extremely accurate one?
What other methods might be more accurate?

What Do You Think?

What are the advantages and disadvantages of a sundial?

Finding the Answer

1. Construct a sundial of wood or aluminum. The gnomon, which casts the shadow, can be a right-angled triangle with the base angle equal to the latitude of the place where you live. The hypotenuse should point to the north star when the hours are being marked on the base piece. Ask your math teacher about right-angled triangles.
2. Experiment to see if your sundial can be calibrated to time units smaller than one hour. For example, try to indicate half hours, quarter hours and minutes.
3. Observe and record the time for several days. Make comparisons with the clocks in your house.
4. Discover when sundials were widely used and when clocks were invented and finally mass-produced.

Showing Your Answers at the Science Fair

1. Show your sundial and indicate its method of construction.
2. Exhibit a chart which shows the origin and historic development of the sundial and other important timekeeping devices.
3. Display a chart which shows the advantages and disadvantages of the sundial in our modern world.

New Questions

How is the accuracy of clocks tested by our city, state and federal governments?

Why is timekeeping important?

What Do You Think?

How do an almanac's long-range predictions compare with those of the U.S. Weather Bureau?

Finding the Answer

1. Purchase an almanac or borrow one from your local library.
2. Record the predictions of the almanac in a vertical column on a sheet of paper or cardboard.
3. Consult the U.S. Weather Bureau's predictions in a local newspaper daily and record this information in an adjoining column on the paper or cardboard.
4. Compare the predictions and note how many times there was complete agreement, partial agreement and no agreement. Note also how many times the prediction was too general or not specific enough to make a comparison.
5. Consult local newspaper files for accounts of one or two severe local storms. Discover if they were predicted by the almanac or the weather bureau.

Showing Your Answers at the Science Fair

1. Exhibit an almanac or a drawing of one and some samples of weather maps. Mount these on a panel of cardboard. Indicate the meaning of the symbols on the maps.
2. Show your chart comparing the predictions of the almanac and those of the weather bureau.
3. Present in writing your evaluation of the two systems of prediction.

New Questions

Of what value are weather predictions?

Why are long-range predictions for a small community or local area often inaccurate?

What Do You Think?

How can we measure changes in air pressure?

Finding the Answer

1. Construct a bottle barometer. Cork a small-necked bottle tightly after a straw has been inserted snugly through the cork and the bottle has been partly filled with water. This barometer will record pressure changes if the temperature is uniform. Otherwise, it will operate as a thermometer. Use wax or candle tallow to seal the cork and straw.
2. Note changes in pressure over a two- or three-week period. Compare your records with readings from a commercial barometer. Also, check weather bureau predictions and records.

Showing Your Answers at the Science Fair

1. Exhibit your barometer and indicate how it was assembled.
2. Make a chart showing your readings of the bottle barometer. Indicate also on the chart the important weather changes which actually occurred during this period. Indicate storms, rain and snowfall.
3. Present in writing your understanding of air-pressure changes and how they are measured.

New Questions

How and why does air pressure change?

How are professional barometers constructed and calibrated?

What Do You Think?

How much is air polluted in my own neighborhood?

Finding the Answer

1. Secure a large strip of white cotton felt or batting. Tack it to a board and cover four-fifths of the cotton-covered board with another board. Each day uncover another one-fifth of the cotton. Observe how the visible impurities increase each day. Determine the apparent density of the polluting elements by examining each section of the cotton under a magnifying glass and comparing them.

The white cotton tacked to the board as shown here will give you a visual measurement of the amount of polluting elements in the air. Just uncover another section of the cotton each day. Check density with a magnifying glass.

2. After a snowstorm, collect one quart of snow and, after allowing it to melt, filter it through a fine mesh cloth. Do this on several days, if possible. Compare the accumulation of polluting elements.
3. Write to your nearest air-pollution control center for information on local air pollution.
4. Investigate any past periods of smog that have occurred in your locality.

Showing Your Answers at the Science Fair

1. Take some photographs of things which cause the air to become polluted. Include chimney smoke, auto exhaust, rubbish fires, etc. Exhibit these photos on a large sheet of cardboard. Indicate their significance as causes of air pollution.
2. Exhibit a chart showing the chemical composition of air and of polluting particles.
3. Show your cotton-felt air-pollution testing device.
4. Present in writing your conclusions about the problem of air pollution in your community.

New Questions

Does air pollution vary much in different localities?

How do some polluting elements, such as strontium 90, become distributed
through the atmosphere around the entire world?

What Do You Think?

How can we measure the speed of wind?

Finding the Answer

1. Construct a simple wind gage or anenometer. Attach four cups to crossed
   sticks so that the center of the opposite cups will be nineteen inches apart.
   Glue the sticks at the center joint and drive a long nail through the joint.
   Loosen the nail by enlarging the hole and place a small washer underneath the sticks.
2. Color one of the cups darker than the others so that it can be easily
   counted as it spins. To find the wind speed count the number of revolu-

This wind-speed indicator was made with four clear plastic cups, four
pieces of one-quarter-inch plywood and a short section of two-by-two.
A long nail and two washers provide the shaft and bearing surfaces.

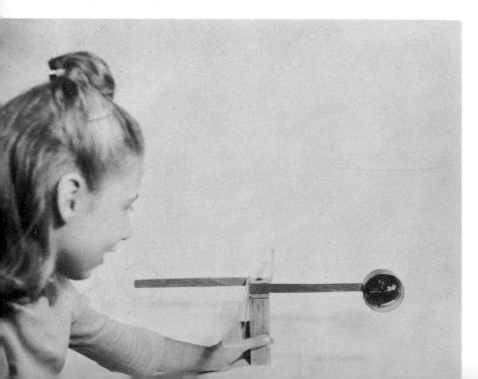

tions per second. Since the cups are moving in a five-foot circle, the speed of the wind may be calculated to be the number of revolutions per second times five. This of course will tell you the speed per second in feet. The miles-per-hour figure may easily be figured from this.

3. Record the wind speeds every day at the same time for a number of days. Check your findings with those of the weather bureau as broadcast or printed in the papers.

Showing Your Answers at the Science Fair

1. Exhibit your wind-speed indicator and tell how it was made and used.
2. Present a chart which shows your own wind-speed measurements and those of the weather bureau.
3. Explain in writing what you have done and how you think wind speed affects weather changes.

New Questions

Why are wind-speed forecasts sometimes unreliable?
What factors determine wind speed?

What Do You Think?

What is the real size and appearance of the human heart and how does it function?

Finding the Answer

1. Investigate to determine the size and location of the human heart. This information can be found in many general reference books, and a visit to a museum where life size replicas of human organs are displayed will be useful. The school nurse, your science teacher and your own doctor may also have some literature on this.
2. Discover the function of the auricles, the ventricles, valves, arteries, and veins. Check with your teacher or a physician about your understanding of the functioning of these organs.

Showing Your Answers at the Science Fair

1. Mount on a painted wooden panel your clay or plaster model of the human heart. Make the model as near to the average size of a heart as possible. Paint the various parts of the heart different colors so they may be easily identified. Indicate the names of the parts and their functions.
2. Explain in writing how you proceeded and what you have discovered.

New Questions

How does a doctor check your heart's functioning?
What may cause your pulse rate to change?

This eighth grader, Craig Fuller, is shown with a model of the heart which was made with clay. It shows the auricles and ventricles as well as the connecting arteries and veins. Direction of flow is indicated.

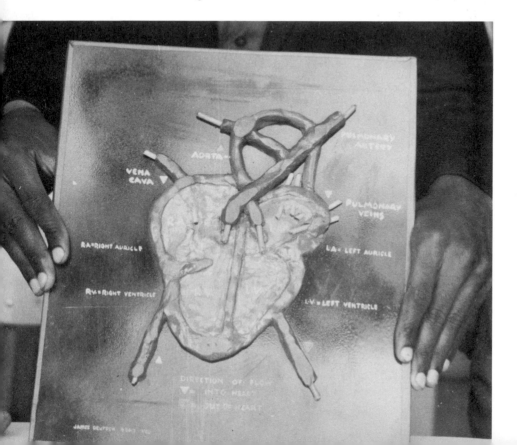

What Do You Think?

What role do the kidneys play in excretion?

Finding the Answer

1. Investigate the structure of the kidney. You can get a fair idea of this organ's structure by examining a veal or lamb kidney. These may be secured from a butcher, of course. Cut the kidney open and look for the tiny tubular structures inside.

2. Discover the role of the tubules in the kidneys and also the ureters which connect the bladder with the kidneys. This information may be found in most biology books. Also check with a science teacher and a physician on the accuracy of your concepts.

3. Find the exact location of the kidneys, ureters and bladder in the human body. These parts of the body are often pictured in biology and other reference books.

Showing Your Answers at the Science Fair

1. Make a clay or plaster model of this part of the body's excretory system. Mount the models of the kidneys and its connected ureters and bladder on a large wooden panel. Label each organ and part and indicate its function.

2. Present in writing exactly what you have done and what you have learned about the role of the kidneys.

New Questions

Can humans get along with only one kidney?
Why are the arteries and veins connected to the kidneys so large?

What Do You Think?

What are living cells like and how do they reproduce?

Finding the Answer

1. Study the ameba and the paramecium. They are one-celled animals which live in stagnant water. The ameba is especially large and is there-

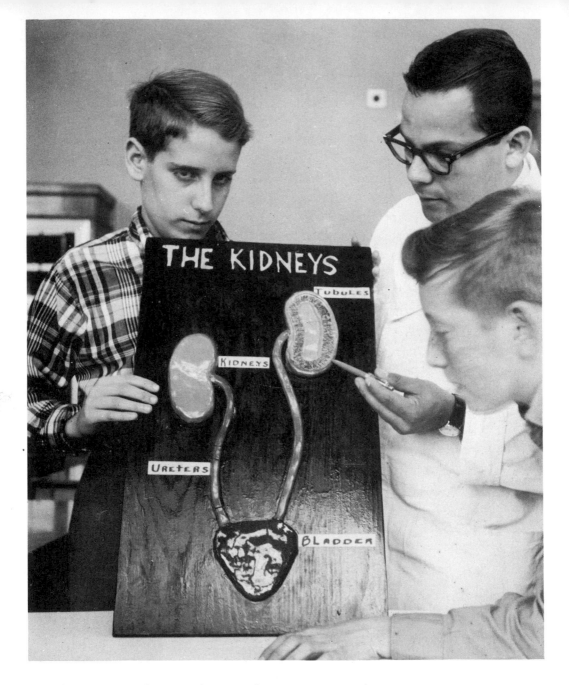

Here the science teacher, Mr. Sheran, is shown pointing out the structure of the kidneys and their connection with the bladder. The models were made of clay and mounted on plywood. Note the black paint and white letters.

fore easier to study. Ask a science teacher to show you one under a microscope or to show you pictures and drawings of ameba. These pictures are easily found in reference books. Parameciums are easy to secure. Boil a handful of hay and several wheat seeds in about two glasses of water. Let this boiled mixture stand for a couple of days in a jar and then add some pond water. In a week or ten days the water should be full of protozoa, including paramecium. Study these under the microscope.

2. Discover what activities go on in a single-celled animal. Learn how it moves about in response to irritation and how it secretes, digests, absorbs and reproduces. Check your discoveries with the information you find in biology books and with your teachers.

3. Investigate what is meant by the "cell doctrine."

Showing Your Answers at the Science Fair

1. Make a series of clay models of the ameba and the paramecium. Indicate the common parts of these animals and show how they reproduce.

2. Explain in writing everything you have done and what you have discovered about living cells.

New Questions

In what ways are the single-celled animals like the cells in the human body? How are plant and animal cells alike?

What Do You Think?

How can fish be conditioned?

Finding the Answer

1. Divide a fish tank into two parts with a piece of glass. Place a Siamese fighting fish or an angelfish or a barb on one side of the partition, and a young guppy on the other side. Now feed the fighting fish some live tubifex worms which can be purchased in most pet stores. Live Daphnia may also be used. After one month remove the glass partition and see if the natural tendency of the fighting fish to attack the guppy has been conditioned. What changes have occurred?

2. Try this experiment using other fish and other foods. Record the time, date and results of each trial.

Showing Your Answers at the Science Fair

1. If possible, exhibit a small tank with a partition. Also exhibit either the fish used or pictures of the fish and the foods.
2. Display a chart which shows the number of trials conducted in each experiment and the results observed.
3. Summarize in writing exactly what you have discovered about the conditioning of fish.

New Questions

What is the fish brain and nervous system like?
Can inherited tendencies be permanently conditioned or changed?

What Do You Think?

How can a tomato plant be grafted to a potato plant?

Finding the Answer

1. Place a potato and a tomato plant in separate pots but close together. When they are about ten inches tall slice off enough tissue from each stem to expose a few vascular bundles. Make the slices on the side of the stems about a third of the distance from the top of the plants. Tie the sliced parts of the stems together using raffia or a similar material. Cover the sliced and wrapped area with paraffin or grafting wax.
2. After a month's time, cut off the tomato stem below the graft and the potato stem above the graft. Observe what happens next. Watch the plants carefully.
3. Discover the source of water for the tomato leaves and the source of food for the potato stem. Will the grafted plant produce potatoes or tomatoes?

Showing Your Answers at the Science Fair

1. Display your grafted plants and indicate how the graft was accomplished.
2. Show a chart which presents a timetable for each step of the process.
3. Exhibit drawings of other methods of grafting.

4. Present in writing the details of what you have done and what you think were the results.

New Questions

What is the value of grafting?
Can any plant be grafted to any other plant?
How do we get seedless oranges and grapefruits?

What Do You Think?

What are fossils and why do scientists study them?

Finding the Answer

1. Visit your local museum or a large one like the American Museum of Natural History in New York. Examine the fossil exhibits.
2. Look for the definition of the word "fossil" in an encyclopedia and a dictionary. Ask your nearest museum or conservation department for information about where to look for fossils. Some state conservation departments publish maps which show areas where fossil remains of certain periods may be found.
3. Locate a fossil yourself, if possible, and try to identify its nature and origin. Use reference books in the library for this purpose.

Showing Your Answers at the Science Fair

1. Exhibit the fossils you have found or photographs of other fossils. Drawings may also be used.
2. With drawings and photographs show the work of the paleontologist and others. Explain the meaning of the word "fossil" and why scientists study them.

New Questions

How long ago did living things first appear on earth?
What are the latest theories about the age of the earth?

The mastodon bones being uncovered here were found in Hackensack, New Jersey, by two high school students. Other students here are from Fairleigh Dickinson, Princeton, Columbia and the City College of New York. They are helping to uncover the fossils.

What Do You Think?

What does a nuclear reactor look like and what is its function?

Finding the Answer

1. Write to the Brookhaven National Laboratory at Upton, Long Island, New York, or any other laboratory where reactors are located. Ask for photographs to illustrate your science project paper.
2. Consult books dealing with atomic fission and other references in the library. Ask your science teacher for references in your school library.
3. Discover the meaning of such words as radioisotope, radioactivity, geiger counter and curies.

Showing Your Answers at the Science Fair

1. Exhibit photographs and drawings of an atomic pile or nuclear reactor. Secure this from a national laboratory or from a newspaper or magazine story.
2. Explain in writing exactly what you have learned about nuclear reactors and their function.

These ice-age mammoths and mastodons once roamed over many parts of the United States. The ones shown here are on display at the New York State Museum in Albany, New York. Where do similar creatures still live?

New Questions

What types of scientists and technicians are employed where nuclear reactors are used?

How does one become a nuclear physicist, for example, and secure employment in a nuclear laboratory?

What Do You Think?

What are the height, weight and thrust of a modern rocket, such as the Atlas, Saturn and the Nova?

Finding the Answer

1. Discover the answers to these questions in space technology magazines and books in the library.
2. Write to the National Aeronautics and Space Administration at the George C. Marshall Space Flight Center in Huntsville, Alabama, for information about the Saturn and Nova programs.

This is the north face of the nuclear reactor at Brookhaven National Laboratory in Upton, New York. The technician on the left uses tongs to remove a newly produced radioisotope from the pneumatic tube system. The physicist at the right is using a survey meter containing a geiger counter.

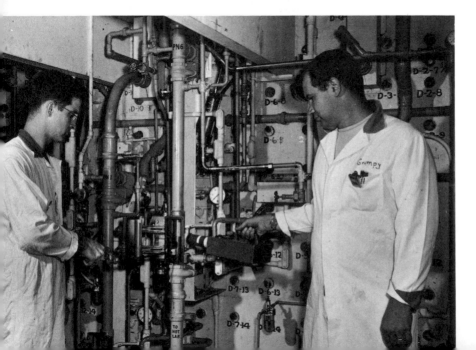

Here is an Atlas missile on its launching platform as the gantry service tower is moved a short distance away. This is a common sight at Cape Kennedy in Florida. Compare the size of the missile with the men at the lower right.

Showing Your Answers at the Science Fair

1. Make cardboard or light wood models of the various rockets to approximate scale. Indicate the various parts or sections of each rocket and the vital information concerning size, weight and thrust.

2. Make a large drawing of each rocket to show its relative size. Draw several of them on a single sheet of cardboard. List also any related information you may have.

3. Make and display small clay models to an approximate scale. Mount four or five of these on a single board and include the appropriate information concerning size and power.

New Questions

How much bigger is a Saturn rocket than a bus or a train?

How does the power or thrust of a rocket compare with the horsepower of an automobile?

WORKING SAFELY

If you're willing to spend a few minutes planning your work and you don't mind asking for help, you can safely make any project in this book. Planning simply means that you decide what you are going to do first, second, third, and so on. Usually, you'll want to assemble all of your materials first. If you can get all of the things you'll need and have them ready in one spot before you go on to the second step, you'll be able to work much more calmly and safely. If you can't get all of the things you need, of course you will want to choose another project.

It's also a good idea to have someone, preferably an adult, check your plan before you start. He or she may have some suggestions which will make your work easier as well as safer. He may even help you to secure some of the things you'll need. Most science projects, even those done by brilliant scientists, are done with some help from others.

Allow yourself plenty of time too. Rushing or hurrying not only leads to accidents but often results in poor work. When you have less time to work, plan to accomplish less. In this way you'll not only do better work but you will suffer fewer bruises, bumps and burns.

Find a good place to work, if you can. Choose a spot where you can leave your tools and materials and know they will not be disturbed. Perhaps there is a spot in your attic or basement where there is enough light and room for a worktable. Occasionally, a garage can be used. If you work in the kitchen remember that you'll have to clean up and put things away before the cook in your family has to do her job.

Remember to protect your clothes too. Loose clothes can also be dangerous. Roll up your sleeves, remove your necktie and, of course, wear an apron.

For additional safety remove any small, loose rugs from the floor before you start to work. Pick up any toys, scrap wood, or other objects which might cause you to stumble. Taking a spill with a tool of some kind in your hand is no fun.

Finally, don't hesitate to ask for help or for information about a tool or procedure you're not sure about. Most teachers, parents and mechanics will be glad to help you.

INDEX

156

157

NOTES

NOTES

The Author

WILLIAM MOORE's interest in science projects dates back as far as his own high school science courses. Today, as an industrial arts teacher in the public schools of New York City, he helps boys and girls with school and home science projects. He has become well known for his magazine articles in the field of woodwork, metal craft, and a variety of how-to-do-its. His articles have appeared in *Boys' Life, Popular Science, Mechanix Illustrated,* and the Workshop Issues of *True* Magazine. He has written two books for Putnam, *Here Is Your Hobby: Fishing* and *Here Is Your Hobby: Science Equipment.* Mr. Moore makes his home in Brooklyn, N.Y., with his wife and three children.